Wendy Leebov's

Essentials for Great
Personal Leadership

Wendy Leebov's
Essentials for Great
Personal Leadership

No-Nonsense Solutions
with Gratifying Results

Wendy Leebov, Ed.D.

2008

Health Forum, Inc.
An American Hospital Association Company
CHICAGO

press

Printed in the United States of America—04/08

Cover design by Cheri Kusek

ISBN: 978-1-55648-351-6

Item Number: 042201

Library of Congress Cataloging-in-Publication Data

Leebov, Wendy.
   [Essentials for great personal leadership]
   Wendy Leebov's essentials for great personal leadership : no-nonsense solutions with gratifying results / Wendy Leebov.
      p. cm.
   Includes bibliographical references and index.
   ISBN 978-1-55648-351-6 (alk. paper)—ISBN 978-1-55648-352-3 (alk. paper)
   1. Health services administration. 2. Leadership. I. Title.
RA971.L369 2008
   362.1068—dc22

2007047743

I dedicate this book to my family,

whose heartwarming encouragement, wise counsel, and love have helped me to pursue my enthusiasms and dedicate time and energy to learning and sharing my learning with others. Thank you especially to my partner, Janet Stephanie Kole; my daughter, Nikki Gollub Bank; my stepson, Gabe Kole Steerman; my parents, Mike and Flo Leebov; my sister, Linda Leebov Goldston; my son-in-law, Chaim Bank; and my grandchildren, Moshe, Chasdeya, and Shuey.

Special thanks to my daughter, Nikki, who is my best editor, sounding board, and partner in developing tools to support health care leaders in their endlessly challenging roles.

Contents

List of Figures and Tools

About the Author

Wendy Leebov, Ed.D., is a passionate advocate for creating healing environments for patients, families, and the entire health care team. She has twenty-five years of experience in helping leaders lead effectively and launch and sustain far-reaching strategies that enhance the patient and employee experience.

During two decades of service with the Albert Einstein Healthcare Network in Philadelphia, Wendy most recently held the position of vice president, human resources. She also founded the Einstein Consulting Group, a firm respected for helping more than 300 health care organizations with strategies to achieve care with compassion and leadership effectiveness.

Now an independent consultant on leadership development, the patient experience, and organizational change, Wendy is also a compelling presenter of keynote presentations and designer and facilitator of workshops and learning processes.

Wendy received her bachelor of arts degree in sociology/anthropology from Oberlin College. She earned her master's in education and doctorate in human development from the Harvard Graduate School of Education.

In addition to writing "The Executive Tool Kit" column for *Hospitals and Health Networks OnLine,* Wendy Leebov has written more than ten books for health care leaders, including *The Indispensable Health Care Manager: Success Strategies for a Changing Environment* (with G. Scott), *Health Care Managers in Transition: Shifting Roles for Changing Organizations* (also with G. Scott), *Achieving Impressive Customer Service: Strategies for the Health Care Manager* (with G. Scott and L. Olson), and *Service Quality Improvement: The Customer Satisfaction Strategy for Health Care* (with G. Scott).

Preface

Leading today is nothing short of a sophisticated juggling act, even if your vision, values, and priorities are clear. There are so many customers to please, so many relationships to build, so many competing pressures, so much change, and just so much to do.

Most executives have become advocates for on-the-job, just-in-time learning, because it's so difficult to create time-outs for learning. That's why at-your-desk, on-the-run, online updates are the rage. And that's where *Wendy Leebov's Essentials for Great Personal Leadership* comes in.

The goal: to provide practical, bite-sized tools for swamped, ever-learning executives. The tools help you to take stock of your leadership effectiveness, lead with vision and results, manage your precious time in alignment with your priorities, and build a work culture and environment that bring out the best in the caring people who work on your team and throughout your organization.

This book includes columns from *Hospitals and Health Networks OnLine's* regular feature "The Executive Tool Kit." With each chapter, you'll find additional tools never before published to help you to share and apply suggested approaches easily. And you'll find an appendix containing "Additional Resources for Health Care Leaders" to help you further pursue those topics of particular interest.

Health care leadership has become a feat of vision, courage, tenacity, and wisdom. Here's hoping these tools will help you to *be* more effective and also to *feel* more gratified in this endlessly challenging role.

Wendy Leebov, Ed.D.
Philadelphia

Wendy Leebov's

Essentials for Great
Personal Leadership

Chapter 1

• • •

Walking the Leadership Tightrope

Effective leaders must learn how to be empathetic, supportive bosses while influencing staff members to make necessary and often difficult changes.

The only sign you can hang on your organization permanently is one that reads "Subject to Change without Notice." The health care environment continues to face massive upheaval triggered by consumer expectations, reimbursement, system formation and dissolution, technology, trends related to quality and safety, worker shortages, the global economy, and much more.

Health care leaders need to actively manage this upheaval unless they want their teams to buckle under the strain. As facilitators of change, leaders walk a tightrope. They must keep their balance in the face of what can be two opposing forces: employees resistant to the change who press their leaders to keep the status quo, and the need to champion new approaches to advance the organization's mission and success strategies.

It is not easy to keep your balance on this tightrope. Four patterns characterize differences among leaders in their stance toward change: victim, critic, observer, and facilitator/advocate.

Four Response Patterns

	Victim	Critic	Observer	Facilitator/ Advocate
Behaviors	• Resists change • Feels angry or depressed • Reverts to old ways • Isolates self • Complains about the process	• Looks for reasons the change will fail • Fails to see potential	• Acts reluctant to get involved • Encourages team to take a "wait and see" attitude • Waits to see what others are going to do	• Looks for ways to minimize negative reactions • Explores reasons for the change • Supports staff • Looks for ways to help • Nurtures people who are affected
Attitudes	• "Can you believe they're doing this to us?" • "Why is this happening to me again?" • "Why can't things stay the same?"	• "This never worked before." • "This won't come about." • "Whose bright idea is this?" • "This will be a flash in the pan."	• "If I ignore this, it will go away." • "I won't jump in until I know it's proven." • "I'm not sticking my neck out on this."	• "This change is an opportunity to do things better." • "While it might need fine-tuning, we can make it work." • "If it doesn't work after we've given it a solid try, we'll learn from that and change our approach." • "I am going to do my part."

Keeping your balance on this tightrope requires you to empathize with and advocate for staff interests while *at the same time* being a positive force in implementing the change for the organization's sake. This is not easy.

A Matter of Design

To ensure effective communication with your team, consider a tactic based on the premise that excellent communication is a matter of design. This planned approach has three components: (1) understanding the big-picture context for the change so well that you can articulate it; (2) coming to terms with your own commitment so you can personally support it; and (3) planning communication tactics that clarify new processes, acknowledge staff feelings, and advance the change rather than hamper it.

It helps to execute the three components in a *conscious* way. Below, each component is described further, along with tools to help your team develop planned approaches to specific changes.

Understand the Big-Picture Context for the Change

Not everyone in a leadership role sees the big picture and how new approaches fit within it. Leaders can't communicate changes effectively or address resistance constructively if they don't fully grasp the context for the changes.

Gather your team together, divide them into small groups (three or so people), and ask them to complete the following worksheet.

The Big Picture: Where Are We? Where Are We Going? Where Do We Fit?

1. **Goals.** What do we see as the main goals of our organization over the next two years?
2. **Challenges.** What are the main challenges ahead?
3. **Current performance.** How are we doing currently in the face of these challenges?
4. **Success strategies.** What are we doing to not only survive but also be successful?
5. **Strengths.** What are the main strengths we have that will help us be successful?
6. **How this team fits.** How do we see our own team contributing to our organization's success strategies?

Then, as a large group, share results and fill in any information gaps. Do this periodically to make sure your teams are constantly updating their knowledge. Then, when you're launching or approaching a specific change, ask the following additional question:

7. **The specific change.** Given where we're going and our strategies for success, how does this change fit into the big picture, and how does it help us succeed in pursuit of our goals?

By engaging your entire management team in discussions of the big picture, you are making sure people share a common-ground understanding of the context for change and can better advance your goals in setting priorities, making decisions, and acting in synchrony.

Come to Terms with Your Own Commitment

A second component of communicating about a change involves the individual. To be effective as a communicator and catalyst for the change, every leader and manager needs to be able to describe the change in positive terms, showing a personal commitment to it.

Leadership Messages in the Event of Change

Inauthentic or uncommitted messages:

- "This is a great idea. Let's go for it!"
- "This is really misguided, but we're expected to cooperate."
- "This too shall pass. In the meantime, please do what needs to be done."

Authentic message that conveys commitment:

"I understand what we're trying to accomplish with this change. While I have some concerns about it, I'm personally prepared to do all I can to make it work, addressing barriers that arise along the way."

This doesn't mean every leader and manager must actively want the change. Leaders should not pretend to be supportive in order to be a team player. Instead, each leader needs to figure out a stance toward the change that will make it possible to wholeheartedly and authentically do what's needed to make it successful with his or her team.

Plan Your Communication Tactics

Assuming that the leader grasps the big picture and has personally come to terms with the change, the third challenge is to create a blueprint for communication that places the change in the big picture, expresses his or her personal commitment, acknowledges concerns, holds the line, and encourages others to join in.

The worksheet that follows helps to synthesize and plan all-important aspects of a change communication.

Planning for Change Communication

	Good Words
Your main message (about a change or new expectation)	
Consequences and benefits (for patients and customers, team, other departments, you, organization)	
Pinch of empathy (acknowledgment of what people might be feeling)	
Repeat and confirm your main message	
Restate your personal commitment (with confidence and optimism and a request for support)	

Example for a Change or Improvement

Your main message	"We are initiating a strategy to improve the quality of teamwork across our organization. I want your full participation."
Consequences and benefits	"When our teamwork falters, we feel the strain, and so do our clients. Things fall through the cracks. People resent each other, and it drains energy from our important work. By strengthening our teamwork, we can become more efficient and more effective and improve the climate here for us as well."
Pinch of empathy	"Now, I realize that our job is intense. We work hard, and sometimes it's not easy to consider how others can help or how we can support them."
Repeat and confirm your main message	"Still, I want us to get on board with our strategy to improve our teamwork."
Restate your personal commitment	"I'm personally convinced it will pay off for us as well as for our patients, and I personally am going to do my part. I hope you'll join me in making this work so we all reap the benefits."

Setting the Stage

The effective leader:

- Seizes opportunities to influence the shape of change and invites staff to provide input
- Comes to terms with the change personally and helps staff do the same
- Plans how to communicate the change in a respectful way that is considerate of employees while advancing the cause of upper management
- Invites reactions and listens with empathy
- Acknowledges resistant feelings without defensiveness and explains further
- Does not join in with or reinforce a *victim* stance
- Calmly holds the line, emphasizing the benefits when the change is non-negotiable
- Role-models resilience and demonstrates that a person can embrace and lead a change without being gung-ho about it
- Shifts focus from "why we can't" to "how we can"
- Shows personal ownership and investment while respecting the feelings and concerns of the team

When managing change, effective leaders manage themselves.

• • •

Additional Tools

Tool 1
THREE TOOLS FOR KEEPING YOUR BALANCE

Because of the endless challenges you face as a health care leader, you are never finished. There is always more to do. It's easy to burn out from overwork and endless pressure. Yet, if you lose your balance and allow work to overwhelm your other priorities in life—relationships, interests, physical fitness, families, learning, recreation, and hopes for the future—you're likely to feel depleted, disaffected, and even cynical. These feelings drain your energy for work and your everyday effectiveness, both at work and outside of work.

Also, when you lose work-life balance, this sends a message to your team. "Who needs this?" they'll ask themselves. "Is this the job for me?"

Here are three tools that help you and your team keep your balance on the leadership tightrope.

1. Inspire Work-Life Balance through Personal Example

Communicate these attitudes through your personal approach to your work and your life. Be blunt. Make the following points explicit to your team, and your team will appreciate you more than you know:

- "I am more than my job. And so are you."
- "I can set limits on my work so I have a life. And so can you."
- "I deserve a break during the day so I can relax and refresh. And so do you."
- "There's more to life than work for me and for you."
- "It's healthy for all of us to have fun at work."
- "I can take my work seriously while also taking myself lightly."
- "I realize I might sometimes drive you to exceed your limits for work, discouraging you from the work-life balance you seek. I'm sorry. I appreciate your help in setting reasonable limits. I want you to feel productive, gratified, and satisfied here. I realize that while this will, I hope, be good for you, it will also be good for the organization."

2. Build Respect for Work-Life Balance within Your Team

Take people by surprise at a leadership meeting by proposing this heartwarming and enlightening team-building exercise:

- State your purpose: You want to find out more about each other's priorities as a basis for strengthening team relationships.
- Ask people to consider this question: "Imagine a wonderful ninety-fifth birthday party for you. What would you hope to hear in people's testimonials about you and your life?" Suggest that people jot down a few messages.
- After a few minutes of reflection, listen to each person's imaginings.
- Afterward, ask the group:
  —"What themes or patterns emerged?"
  —"What implications do you see for our work together?"

Inevitably, issues related to work-life balance will surface, and people can discuss how to help each other take on reasonable, healthy work commitments that will enable them to live according to their dreams.

3. Keep Perspective by Learning Endlessly

Ask yourself the following questions, and build your team by engaging it in addressing these as well:

- To what extent do I stay in my comfort zone?
- What have I learned lately?
- How will I seek further information and feedback?
- How much time do I spend learning?
- When was the last time I created an experiment so I could learn from the experience?
- How do I take advantage of informal learning opportunities?
- What can I learn that will renew me?

Tool 2
COACHING ON COACHING

To help the people around you advance the organization's priorities, you will need to play the role of coach. You can't call every shot or do every task. There is simply far too much to do. Your only hope lies in developing the capacities and competencies of the people around you, creating a multiplier effect in terms of organizational capability.

Are you an effective coach? Assess your coaching attitudes and behaviors using these ten tips.

1. **Ask questions.** Help managers share more by asking open-ended questions rather than yes-no ones. Talk less and question more.
2. **Don't judge.** People shut down if they feel criticized or labeled. Make sure you state your feedback and observations constructively.
3. **Listen carefully.** Try to absorb the meaning behind the words. Ask people to explain to be sure you understand. "Tell me more" is a nonthreatening way to get people to elaborate.
4. **Maintain an open mind.** Suspend disbelief; try to understand the manager's approach if it differs from yours. Give people space to experiment and learn.
5. **Praise and build on their ideas.** "Yes!" and "Good idea!" encourage people to continue the dialogue.

6. **Focus on the person.** Talk about yourself and your experiences sparingly. You won't develop others by talking about yourself at length.

7. **Slow down.** People won't open up if they feel rushed. Most people need time to assemble their thoughts, feelings, and ideas.

8. **Eliminate distractions.** Managers will not feel valued if you are doing other things when you are supposed to be talking with them. Don't let phones, beepers, e-mail alerts, or other people interrupt this protected time.

9. **Less is more.** People can't focus on many instructions or many issues at once. Center each discussion on one or two key topics, and build on them in later discussions.

10. **Be supportive.** Make sure you are not coming across as intimidating or threatening when you offer suggestions. If you want something done in a certain way, make sure you explain how and why. Motivation by fear is notoriously ineffective.

Chapter 2

• • •

Four Ways to Get a Grip

*Better time management, improved concentration,
and breakthrough communication with problem
co-workers can go a long way toward
reducing stress. Here's how to do it.*

Are you and your team running ragged? Do you feel there are too many priorities, there is too much to do, and there is not enough time? You may think, "I don't have time to learn how to deal with stress effectively," but that thought can kill you.

If you're on a treadmill of stress, overload, and exhaustion, you can be sure you're paying a price. Maybe you're becoming inefficient and drained from the unrelenting pressure and angst. You might be getting flack from your loved ones who are worried about you, feel shortchanged, or feel neglected. And perhaps you're beating yourself up because you realize your work is interfering with your health and your family's well-being.

After attending an embarrassing number of stress management programs and reading a huge array of stress management books, I have finally succeeded in getting a grip in my own life by successfully applying four specific strategies. Enthusiastic from my long-awaited success, I want to share these four strategies with you. The wonderful thing about them is that you have the power to apply them whether the people around you are supporting you or not. Of course, it's much easier if they cooperate, but, with determined self-discipline, you can make headway even if they don't.

Four Ways to Get a Grip

> - Focus
> - Flow
> - Reflection
> - Courageous conversations

Focus

Have you seen a chest of drawers with many, many little drawers? If you put stuff in all of those drawers and pull out all the drawers at once, the chest of drawers loses its balance and falls forward. If, instead, you open one drawer at a time, then push each one back in before you move on to the next, the chest keeps its balance, and you don't get dizzy from all the demands for your attention.

Your time is that chest of drawers. See if you can pull out one drawer at a time, allowing yourself to focus on one task fully, then close the drawer before you pull out another.

> To focus:
>
> - Pull out one drawer at a time.
> - Deal with it to your satisfaction.
> - Push it back in.
> - Once you've pushed it back in, let go of it.

Flow

Multitasking has become valued. Yet some researchers claim that doing more than one task at a time is not possible. They say that people are not really doing two things at once. Instead, they are making rapid shifts in attention from one thing to another. At any moment, only one thing is getting the attention. And each time you shift your attention, you lose efficiency. People known to be good at multitasking are really rapid shifters. People who think they're multi-taskers typically feel frustrated, as they have trouble finishing anything or achieving closure, and the rapid shifts in attention can feel dizzying, like a way-too-fast table tennis game.

Flow is the second strategy for getting a grip. Flow and multi-tasking do not peacefully coexist. According to psychologist Mihaly Csikszentmihalyi, professor at Claremont (CA) Graduate University and a noted researcher, *flow* is a mental state in which you are completely absorbed in what you are doing and feeling energized, fully engaged, and successful in the process.

Imagine that you need to move your refrigerator from the kitchen to the basement, but it's too heavy. You find help by locating two strong people who agree to move your refrigerator downstairs for you. Now imagine that they are midway down the stairs, grunting and puffing, as they move the heavy appliance gingerly down the steps. At this moment, would you butt in? Would you say, "Hey, buddy, how about a soda?" "Hey guys, look over here for a minute!" No, you would have to be nuts to interrupt them at that moment. They could lose their balance, drop the refrigerator, hurt themselves, dent the floor, get stuck, and who knows what else. You would not think about interrupting them in the midst of their challenging task. You would not dare to interrupt their "flow."

When you have tough work to do and you are struggling to do it, do you allow yourself and others to break your concentration? As a health care executive, you are doing plenty of heavy lifting. You run tremendous risks, and frustrate yourself, when you engage in quick stops and starts.

To achieve flow:

- If you have a time limit, set a timer to go off when you need to stop.
- Watching the clock will interfere with your flow.
- Breathe.
- Focus.
- Concentrate. Bring your awareness fully to the task at hand. Become "present" to it. Stop thinking about what you were just doing and what you need to do later. Savor the present moment. Experience fully what you are doing.
- If other thoughts enter in, notice them and let them go.
- Keep breathing and stay with it.

Reflection

Are you programmed to think, "Don't just sit there. Do something!"? If so, you probably do too much and think too little. This kind of approach gives people a reputation as "the roadrunner."

The roadrunner speeds through many responsibilities at a fast clip, stirring up dust and sweating in the process. Does this sound like you? Or do you feel like you're on automatic pilot, rushing from one thing to the next as different demands and needs command your attention?

If either of these roadrunner types characterizes you, you run risks. You might be rushing, rushing, rushing, doing the wrong things, because you didn't consciously decide what most warrants your attention. You might be leaving dust in your wake; you might be straining relationships, hitting unforeseen roadblocks, or missing out on choice points as you cut corners to get to the goal faster.

Build reflection into your day. Schedule quiet time to think and regain your composure and your sense of balance. You'll improve your efficiency; refresh your mind; and make better, more thoughtful decisions. Call it a meeting or a doctor's appointment—or "checkup" or "efficiency committee meeting"—and schedule it. If you spend 1 percent of your day (fifteen minutes) centering yourself and reflecting, this will have a profoundly positive effect on the other 99 percent of your day.

To reflect:

- Breathe. Relax yourself. Unplug.
- Push your "clear" button.
- Recall your mission and purpose.
- Feel your feeling.

Courageous Conversations

Do you find yourself working around people you find difficult or resistant? Do you figure out workarounds when you don't want to deal with them or you've given up? Do you do twice the work because others aren't doing theirs? Are you personally filling gaps and addressing needs because there doesn't seem to be anyone else to do so? Are you avoiding talking about the elephants in the room, the undiscussables?

These conditions aggravate burnout in a big way. The remedy: courageous conversations. Create a dance card for yourself. List the people whom you are allowing to hold you back, slow you down, or irritate you. Determine to have one courageous conversation a week to see if you can influence the dynamics for the better.

To prepare for a courageous conversation:

- Check in with yourself first. What are you bringing to the situation? Do you have sensitivities, history, biases, or unspoken hopes or expectations that might be influencing the situation?
- What do you genuinely respect or admire about this person? If you can get in touch with that, you will be able to have a much more constructive and respectful conversation.
- Can you let go of feelings of anger, frustration, or hopelessness so that you can shift to an inquiry or a discovery mode? Ask yourself what might be contributing to the other person's behavior.

Then open the conversation with a positive statement of your intent, such as, "I want a really good work relationship with you. I want to explore ways we might be more effective partners when we share goals and priorities."

Use your best feedback skills, including those in the feedback model below.

Feedback Model

Describe the behavior: "When you _____."

Express your feeling: "I feel _____."

Explain the impact/reasons: "Because _____."

Clarify what you want: "_____."

"I'm asking that you _____."

"I'll appreciate _____."

"My suggestion is _____."

Of course, you can expect some feedback and response to your message. Receive feedback with grace and thoughtfulness. Persist to reach common-ground agreements. Go into the conversation with an open mind and do the following:

- Assume that the other person also has good intentions.
- Try to stop yourself from becoming defensive, since this will send the conversation off course.
- Remind yourself that the choice is yours about whether you agree with or act on the feedback you're receiving.
- Listen carefully and check your understanding by reflecting back to the person what you heard.
- Adopt an attitude of curiosity. Inquire without judging or interrogating so you can fully understand.
- Summarize your common ground, and invite and propose agreements for the future.

Some people think that executives who live a frenzied life must reap rewards from it or they would find ways to change their everyday experience. But you wouldn't have read this far if you weren't aware, at some level, of the price you're paying for running ragged. You do have options that are within your control.

• • •

Additional Tools

Tool 1
PERSONAL GUIDELINES FOR HANDLING TRANSITION AND CHANGE

In health care, changes are thrown at us from many directions, and we are just expected to adapt. No wonder many of us feel exasperated, exhausted, or confused. While change can become our enemy, by shifting how we orient toward any given change, we can create opportunity—an opening through which we can move and grow.

The following guidelines can help you and your team to acknowledge and embrace a change, thereby unlocking the opportunity for growth inherent within.

1. Talk to a trusted colleague about the losses you feel and the difficulties of "letting go" of the way things used to be.
2. Sit down with your manager and think through the major aspects of the change. Sort out what is important and what is no longer "value-added work" as it relates to your (their) own job.
3. Make space in your life to grieve the loss without judging yourself.
4. Make a short list of the "new realities," and test your list with a colleague experiencing the same change. Express your feelings about the change and how it is affecting you. Thank the listener for listening.
5. Spend time learning more about the change and outcomes expected by talking to your manager and co-workers to clarify their vision.
6. With a trusted colleague, think through how your interests and skills fit and support the change.
7. Consider ways you can extend yourself and expand your skills.
8. Work together with your boss to clarify new expectations and development plans to position you for the future.
9. Express interest in joining in to plan the change and its aftermath.
10. Make yourself visible as an advocate for the change.
11. Work with your leader to prepare a step-by-step plan for phasing in the change and your changing role.
12. Share enthusiasm for the change with your leader and your team.
13. Share positive dynamics and effects you see as the change takes hold.
14. Take action to achieve quick successes under the new way or changed circumstances. Help to convince the doubters.

Tool 2
YOUR PERSONAL "BALANCE" SCORECARD

The following simple accounting, attended to frequently, can help you gracefully navigate your many responsibilities and goals with a sense of balance and awareness. Spend five minutes a day auditing today's activities and tomorrow's calendar to make sure you are allocating your time to the key roles important to you in your life. By allocating time daily to each of these key roles, you will feel harmony with your values and priorities and avoid losing your balance.

My Balance Scorecard

Key roles important to me (e.g., partner, parent, professional, leader, coach, activist, healthy person, relationship builder)	Reflected in today's activities?	Reflected in my schedule for tomorrow?	Good news? Bad news? Resolution/ new commitment?
Leader			

Chapter 3

• • •

Inviting the Soul to Work

*Many employees choose to work in a hospital
because they want to make a difference.
Use that motivation to energize and inspire them.*

Many of us have led the charge to provide consistently great and memorable service experiences for patients and families. As we attempt to create a *wow* experience, it becomes ever clearer that demoralized employees are never going to make great service a reality.

At the same time, we are suffering from acute worker shortages; we watch with a sense of powerlessness as previously dedicated, now cynical, employees jump ship to find what they believe will be more satisfying work.

In the human quest for meaning, health care work can be a blessing. It offers opportunities every day to make a difference. But sadly, our precious associates are losing heart and running out of steam. This is made so by a combination of internal and external forces:

- Too much work, leading to exhaustion
- Not enough time
- Dizzying change
- Routines that become routine
- Strained relationships
- Topics that people need to discuss but don't
- Isolation and task orientation at the expense of fun and communication
- Poor management attitudes such as, "Employees are replaceable," "Money is everything," "We need workhorses," and "My way or the highway"

- Tolerance for whining, disrespect, and *attitude*
- Lack of personal acknowledgment and meaningful recognition
- And so much more

So where does that leave us as leaders who want a motivated, inspired, and engaged workforce?

Finding the Soul

The time is now to rekindle the soul at work. *Soulful* work is key to employee satisfaction and retention. And wonderfully, it is *also* a key to further enhancing patient and family satisfaction.

Engage your leadership team in addressing this challenging issue. Devote a meeting to thinking together about what constitutes soulful work and how you can use your power as leaders to create the environment and conditions that pull for it throughout your workforce.

Meeting Agenda

There have been times when you've felt your soul fully engaged at work. These are precious moments when high performance and high fulfillment come together. You experience a "good tired."

Share a time when your soul was fully engaged. Tell us the story.

- Having heard each other's stories, what themes or patterns did you hear from one story to another? List these.
- Now, knowing the factors that need to be present to engage us fully, how can we create more of these so that we engage our employees more fully and soulfully?

Some Thoughts on the Matter

Soul. What does it mean? Aliveness? Spirit? Authenticity? Compassion? Heart? Wholeheartedness? Inspiration? A yearning for deep engagement? While it's not easy to define, we all know it when we see it. And we know it when we feel it. Soul is our basic life energy, to work and live, on purpose—with joy, vitality, and authenticity. Soul is the inspiration of the artist, the drive of the entrepreneur, the curiosity of the scientist, the pride of a parent, the drive of the health care professional to be of help. When we experience soul in our work, we bring our whole selves to work, applying our life energy to the mission of the job *and* our everyday *process* or experience of doing that job.

So, how can we as leaders foster soulful work? Poet David Whyte said in his book *Crossing the Unknown Sea* (Riverhead, 2002), "The antidote to exhaustion is not rest. It is wholeheartedness." We can foster wholeheartedness. We can rekindle the meaning of the work, highlighting people's contributions. We can support ongoing learning so people feel refreshed and refueled. And we can build community so people feel a sense of belonging.

This leads me to what I call the three Cs of soulful work:

- *Contribution:* Does what I'm doing matter?
- *Craft:* Am I into it? Am I getting better at it all the time?
- *Community:* Am I connected to people in an authentic way?

Contribution

We all want to make a difference. We have *succeeded* in teaching that health care is a business. We have succeeded to the detriment of our staff, so many of whom feel robbed of their sense of contribution as we focus them on sacred numbers instead of sacred encounters.

We need to create arenas in which we all tell our stories of making a difference.

Monthly Staff Meeting

- Take a few minutes to jot down some notes about one time this month when you really felt like you made a difference and it meant something to you. Prepare to tell the whole story.
- Form groups of four people and have them share their stories with each other.
- Then, with the full group, ask, "What impressed you as you listened?"
- Close by expressing your admiration for people and the difference they're making. Tell them that next month, you'll be asking for more stories.

Knowing we'll be called upon to share our *contribution stories,* we are more likely to note the experiences when they're happening. We are more likely to appreciate ourselves at that moment, and we are more likely to relive these satisfying times later with a renewing effect.

Craft

Craft is about enjoying the journey, intensely experiencing our work moment to moment. Martin Luther King, Jr., said in his book *The Measure of a Man* (Augsburg Fortress, 2001), "If you are called to sweep streets, but you sweep them the way Beethoven wrote music, you will never have an unhappy day in your life." How can we become this absorbed in our work process when we have our to-do lists running through our heads, making it seemingly impossible to savor even one precious moment of contact with a patient? We need to engage our teams in discussions that will help all of us deepen our sense of craft.

Discussion Questions to Deepen Our Sense of Craft

- What can we do to turn our everyday transactions with patients into sacred encounters?
- How can we control interruptions so we create space for each other to have meaningful moments with our patients and other customers?
- How can we call attention to the parts of our work process that feel gratifying and move the focus away from the frustrations and the constraints?

A sense of craft is also about learning. What's inside of us wants to grow. Don't let this spark go out.

Promote Sharing of Learning Wish Lists

Starting with your team, invite people to share their learning wish list so people can help each other make it happen.

Ask: What have you learned in the last year that makes you feel better about how you do your work?

Then ask: What could you learn that would nourish your life at work?

Ask every person on your team to have this same discussion at a meeting with their direct reports, and they in turn with theirs, creating a cascade of learning dreams and mutual support.

Community

This is all about belonging—within the work team, the community, the family, the world. Given all the waking hours we devote to our demanding jobs, it would be quite alienating to feel like an outsider. As leaders, we can help people connect to each other in meaningful ways by doing such things as:

- Devoting work time to building relationships
- Making it safe to speak openly about real issues
- Creating rituals and celebrations that bind people together and remind people of each other's value
- Becoming facilitators of dialogue instead of being downward communicators

Quick Community Building

Spend five minutes per meeting building relationships and a sense of community. Bring people closer together. Ask them to complete one sentence starter per meeting, such as

- I really feel proud when . . .
- If I were to receive a magic box at the post office, I wish it would contain . . .
- A strength I bring to work that others might not know about is . . .
- What I appreciate about this team is . . .
- What I appreciate about you is . . .

By making a difference, savoring the moments that make the work meaningful, and creating a sense of belonging, you can foster soulful work for you and your employees. The results will be an exceptional employee experience and an exceptional patient experience. And your staff will be proud of their contribution to this remarkable environment.

• • •

Additional Tools

Tool 1
HOW TO TRIGGER THE SHARING
OF SOUL-TOUCHING STORIES

Health care professionals are so busy and task oriented these days, it's not unusual for them to lose touch with their original mission of helping people. And when they lose touch with their once-energizing mission, they run the risk of becoming disaffected and disillusioned and are more likely to jump ship.

Help people stay connected to their mission by writing and sharing stories. Institute a system that inspires people to focus less on the frustrations and more on their gratifying experiences at work.

Institute an Ongoing Process

Equip internal people with methods to facilitate story-catching processes for employee renewal. Some organizations have a training professional facilitate story-writing and story-sharing groups. In other organizations, executives run story-sharing sessions, using their power as role models by starting with their own touching stories of gratifying work.

- Convene caregivers in or across teams. Read a story you have written that describes in vivid detail a time when you felt your work was particularly important and meaningful.
- Explain that written stories tend to be richer in detail than spoken stories. Also, once written, stories can be read and reread, and easily shared. Ask people to let go of any resistance to writing—and to allow themselves to recall and let flow on paper all the details about a time when their work was really meaningful to them.
- Ask everyone to take twenty minutes to write about an instance when they felt particularly fulfilled in their work. Tell people not to worry about the quality of their writing—just to let the story flow out of their hand. Remind them to write the story in detail. Alert people that you will then ask them to read their story with a partner.
- After everyone writes their stories, ask them to share with a partner. Then invite volunteers to share their story with the whole group.
- Consider holding an employee show consisting of a mix of people reading their stories. This can be a wonderful nurses' week event.

- Develop a magazine of stories and publish issue after issue. People will be curious to read each other's stories, making the sharing of soul at work positively contagious.
- Build team cohesion and spirit through sharing the gratifying experiences in their work. You will foster positivism in the midst of considerable job pressure.

Distribute an Evaluation Tool for the Story-Catching Process

Recently, you participated in a process that engaged you and your co-workers in writing and sharing important stories. How would you describe your feelings as a result of the story-sharing experience?

Place a check in the box that best describes how you feel.	Strongly agree	Agree	Neither agree nor disagree	Disagree	Strongly disagree
I feel a strong attachment to my co-workers.					
My manager respects the work I do.					
I feel that I really make a difference to patients and their families.					
My work here is satisfying to me.					
This organization attracts and retains outstanding people.					
People here work hard to make this organization a great place to work.					
I really feel like part of a team in my job.					
In my job, I feel recognized as an individual.					
I'm proud to work here.					

This tool can also be distributed before the process begins, and again at its conclusion, to enable managers to compare the results.

Tool 2
SOUL KILLERS AT WORK

Engage your team in discussing these soul killers. Reach agreements about how you will approach each of the following situations if and when it arises:

- Someone is not fulfilling a promise.
- Someone is doing something unethical.
- Roles and responsibilities are unclear.
- You feel ignored by, underused by, unappreciated by, or disappointed in someone you respect.
- You feel overburdened because someone else slacked off.
- You see a better way but think others will resist.
- Your colleague has irritating habits.
- A lot is not being said that, if said, would move people forward.
- There's a discrepancy between what people say and do, and it's affecting you negatively.
- You're afraid of giving bad news because it might demoralize staff.
- You avoid confronting people who behave inappropriately but are loyal to you.
- You need help but fear looking incompetent.
- You want candid feedback but are afraid of looking needy.
- You have positive thoughts about someone but hesitate to give appreciation.
- You want to give someone negative feedback but are afraid it will demoralize him or her.
- You suspect substance abuse in a colleague and are concerned about him or her.
- You're attending meetings that are a waste of time.
- You think you could contribute a great deal to a project, but it's not yours to do.
- _____

Chapter 4

• • •

How Do You Say Thanks?

The single greatest motivator of employees is appreciation. Use it genuinely and frequently, and you'll see performance improve.

Financial powerhouse Charles Schwab said, "I have yet to find the person, however exalted in his or her station, who did not do better work and put forth greater effort under a spirit of approval than under a spirit of criticism" (*Succeeding with What You Have,* Century Press, 1920). In the pressured world of health care, it's an enormous challenge these days to foster high performance while maintaining morale and a spirit of positivism. Recognizing people's contributions, and doing so consistently and effectively, is critical.

Behavioral science surveys conducted periodically since 1945 have asked employees what matters most to their job satisfaction. "Full appreciation for work done," "interesting work," and "being in on things" come in first, second, and third, respectively, while "job security" and "good wages" appear further down the list.

Yet studies on recognition reveal that the only reinforcement employees receive, in their view, is lack of negative feedback. The message they perceive from leaders is, "You apparently performed well enough to keep your job. So you should be grateful and motivated." Employees don't find this message very inspiring.

No Excuses Allowed

Why are many leaders notoriously stingy with recognition? Consider these common excuses:

Excuse	Response
"I don't have time."	It takes two seconds to say "thanks" and a whole lot longer to work with employees who feel unappreciated and resentful.
"It'll go to their heads and they'll get lazy."	This is an outright fallacy. Giving recognition does not cause standards to slide. People who feel appreciated hustle more and treat customers better.
"My boss doesn't recognize me and I perform well anyway!" Or "Good performance is expected! A paycheck is thanks enough."	These excuses reflect a "boot camp" mentality that suggests that people try harder if they have to knock themselves out for a crumb of recognition. Employees resent this attitude and bad-mouth the leaders who display it.
"I don't have enough money to recognize my employees well."	The most effective form of recognition is a pat on the back—face to face or in a short note. Research shows that a pay raise is highly motivating for two weeks only; after that, other workplace factors shape morale.
"Some employees probably feel patronized when I thank them."	People universally appreciate sincere thanks.
"I'm too swamped with problems to notice the good things."	Remember in elementary school when the problem kids got all the attention and the good kids resented it? Failure to recognize positive behavior tends to lessen such behavior. Some people will even resort to negative behavior (or threaten to jump ship) in order to get your attention.
"I can't be everywhere at once to see everything people are doing."	It doesn't all have to come from you. You can engage your team to create a mix of recognition methods that gets recognition flowing from many sources and in many directions.
"I don't know how to recognize staff effectively." Or "I find it personally difficult to say thanks."	Then do something about this. Great books and tool kits abound. It is your responsibility as a leader to manage and inspire performance. Coaching and feedback, including positive feedback, are critical elements.

The Keys to Effectiveness

To ensure that your recognition efforts have positive effects, keep in mind these twelve principles:

Twelve Principles of Employee Recognition: Recognition Tools for the Health Care Manager

1. **Recognition really matters—to people, performance, and your organization.** It says, "I see you. You make a difference. You matter to me and the organization." Lack of recognition is one of the top three reasons given for job flight. More often than not, employees report quitting their supervisor, not their organization.

2. **The most fundamental form of recognition is your attention.** Acknowledge employees as you pass in the hall, listening, showing interest, asking questions, calling them by name, conveying respect, and tuning in to the individual.

3. **Compensation is not an effective recognition method.**
   - People view compensation as a right. They view recognition as a gift.
   - Compensation is largely inflexible once it's set. People come to expect raises. It's rare to lower someone's pay.
   - Cash burns a hole in people's pockets. People spend their raise or bonus, they get used to having it, then they forget about the source or reason.
   - It takes 8 percent of a person's salary to positively affect a person's behavior with cash. That's a lot. If you want to provide tangible rewards, know that rewards that cost far less but have symbolic value are most effective.
   - Effective recognition methods are immediate and flexible. They can occur anytime. You can alter and vary your methods in response to the person, the nature of the positive behavior, the setting, and available resources. Pay is a lot less flexible.

4. **Recognition should be linked to performance.** People should believe that recognition is a direct response to their efforts, not a matter of luck. Effective recognition methods clearly communicate the behavior that triggered it.

5. **We need employees of the moment more than we need employees of the month.** To reinforce positive behaviors, recognize them as soon as possible—the sooner the better.

6. **Recognition should be personal.** When you give everyday recognition, you should be in direct contact with the recipient to jointly savor his or her accomplishments.

7. **Recognition methods should not create winners and losers.**
   - Everyone should be able to win. If one person wins, it shouldn't mean others lose. If an employee-of-the-month program is your primary recognition method, there are far too few winners. You can be sure that throngs of people feel invisible and disregarded as the select few win.
   - Everyone should be eligible. When recognition goes primarily to caregivers, those who support the caregivers feel forgotten and demoralized. Don't neglect people who work nights and weekends.

8. **Employees should participate in determining recognition methods.** Some recognition traditions offend employees month after month, year after year. Invite employees to help shape your methods and programs, and check with employees periodically to assess and improve.

9. **There should be many sources of recognition.** You are but one source. You can also create conditions and supply methods that help co-workers recognize each other, celebrate the team, and recognize others across department lines.

10. **Different strokes for different folks.** A mix of methods is important. Your team can have fun figuring out a great mix, including methods that are informal and formal, planned and spontaneous, serious and whimsical, traditional and novel, simple and effortful.

11. **Consistent excellence is a matter of design.** Whether you're talking about designing services that delight customers, eliminating errors, or providing recognition, your organization and you personally need a *process*. Without a designed process for ensuring frequent, effective, and widespread recognition, you run the risk of forgetting or missing the boat.

12. **You can give recognition even if you're not getting it.** You create the culture you want through your personal performance and initiatives.

The Tools of Appreciation

People have so much on their minds. Prompt leaders to recognize each other by handing out congratulatory notes, making commendations in staff meetings, creating award programs, and implementing other methods. Tools like the following encourage recognition from person to person, team to team, and patient to staff.

Install a commendation process that carries weight. Consequences influence people's behavior. While most organizations have formal disciplinary documents, the absence of a positive counterpart serves only to emphasize the negative. Institute a two-part (one for employee, one for file) commendation form as a standard performance management tool.

Use a reminder notepad. Create a notepad such as the one below and pass it around so everyone can easily give quick thanks.

To:
- ☐ Way to go!
- ☐ Applause!
- ☐ Ta-daah and thanks!
- ☐ Couldn't have done it without you!
- ☐ You're the best!
- ☐ Bravo!

Here's why: _____

_____

With appreciation,

_____

Offer peer awards. Have teams prepare awards for one another and present them publicly. Or invite team members to toast others for laudable actions.

Send thank-you grams. As part of each department's professional recognition week, circulate a form that invites all staff to recognize the department or individuals.

Pass the pickle jar from one department to another. One department gives another department a big pickle jar filled with thanks and a relevant goodie. In one hospital, nursing sent a jar of whistles to environmental services with the appreciation message, "You whistle while you work. Thank you for bringing cleanliness and cheer to our patients." Each month, the jar travels to a new department with an appreciation message and relevant contents.

Institute "A Patient Thinks You're Great!" cards. Make it easy for patients and families to thank staff who made a difference.

A Patient Thinks You're Great!

To: _____

From: _____   Date: _____

Patient Comments:

THANK YOU!

Supervisor: _____   President: _____

Stock a kudos closet: Make available to all managers a kudos closet filled with items they can give to individuals and teams as tokens of appreciation (e.g., certificates, small plastic trophies, stress balls, thank-you Post-It style notepads, coupons for a free beverage in the cafeteria).

Personal Pointers and Accountability

Recognition programs and tools require human energy. This starts with you!

Acknowledge the individual. Communicate in words and deeds, "You, uniquely you, matter to me." Greet each employee with a smile and a hello—and use names. Express interest in each employee's health, family, and interests.

Give constructive feedback. Be specific and behavioral. Define the action that deserves appreciation. Explain how it made a difference. Make it timely: recognize contributions as soon as you become aware of them, not only during performance reviews. Don't mix your message, as in, "I appreciate how hard you work to solve patients' problems. I wish you'd do the same for me!" Don't use recognition to flatter and manipulate people into doing undesirable jobs: "Bob, you're so good at taking notes! Would you please go to this meeting for me again, take good notes, and type them up by the end of the day?" Also, don't use recognition as emotional blackmail: "I fussed over how hard you work, so please stay late and do this for me."

One size doesn't fit all; match your methods to the person. While gregarious employees might want their achievements acknowledged in front of others, introverted people might respond best to a simple memo. One employee might like to have lunch with an administrator, while another would not.

Give people credit. When your employees excel, it reflects positively on you. When discussing employee or group ideas with other people, credit them; make sure they know you make a habit of this.

Give genuine recognition. People have become cynical about perfunctory thank yous. If you don't put thought into the recognition you're giving, applying it to the individual, the effect may be the opposite of what you intended. Use "I," not "we."

Develop a recognition routine so you remember to recognize staff often. Create your own reminder system—a weekly appointment in your personal digital assistant or e-mail or a reminder message on your screen saver or voice mail. You should supplement spontaneous recognition by dedicating a specific time when you'll take stock of recognition given and needing to be given. For instance, in the last five minutes each day or on a Friday afternoon, ask yourself, "What has each person done right/well today (or this week)?" Then jot them a quick note of appreciation.

Recognition starts with you. An American Red Cross leader once said, "Reward is respect made visible." Make visible your respect for the valuable members of your team.

By taking initiative to strengthen recognition within your organization, you send that all-important message: "You matter!" People will appreciate you for it.

• • •

Additional Tools

Tool 1
START YOUR OWN PEACE CORPS

These days, your employees are undoubtedly working hard, dealing with the stresses and strains typical throughout our turbulent health care field. Show respect for the emotional energy and generosity they extend to patients, families, and other customers by providing a "Peace Corps"—a squad of people who acknowledge and ease the stress.

- Organize a squad of volunteers to help caregivers relieve stress, take a refreshing break, or get a few minutes of pampering. Provide mobile neck rubs, lead a stretch break, sing an inspiring song, or put on a humorous skit.
- Create a Peace Corps room with readings and music for meditation and relaxation.
- Build a caregiver library with thought-provoking and supportive poems, articles, and books that shed light on the challenges of being ill.
- Engage staff in getting creative about how the Peace Corps can help them.

Tool 2
DO THIS AND YOUR MANAGERS WILL
GIVE MORE RECOGNITION

Provide every manager with a recognition tool box to make it easy to award employees.

Purchase from a vendor of promotional items several cardboard or plastic tool boxes imprinted with your organization's logo and "My Personal Recognition Tool Kit." Load the kit with quick recognition tools.

Recognition Tool Kit Items

- Blank certificates for a variety of accomplishments, such as being a team player, resolving complaints, going the extra mile, boosting morale, living the organization's values, supporting co-workers, having a good sense of humor, being a star performer, and many more
- Kudos-grams
- Pre-printed stickers
- Business card–size cards printed with "Standing Ovation," "Kudos for You," or "Big Ta-daah!" for managers to keep in their pocket for use during rounding
- Candy bars
- Pre-printed Post-It style praise pads (with phrases such as "Ta-daah!" "Thanks!" "Congrats!" and "You Make a Difference!")
- Trinkets with your organization's logo and thanks (such as pocket mirrors, stress balls, stars, badges)
- A card set of ideas for recognition from which managers can pick and choose

To extend the reach of recognition:

- Engage an employee team to select and design contents for the tool boxes.
- Maintain a closet of supplies and a recognition supplies order form for replenishing supplies when they run out.
- Hold an annual recognition summit for managers during which you engage managers in peer and team recognition activities and a team celebration. During the summit, introduce new contents for the tool boxes for the coming year.

Chapter 5

• • •

Healing a Troubled Relationship

*If two team members are at odds
with each other, wasting time and
sapping energy from the group, insist
that they sit down and talk it out.*

Human nature and individual differences dictate that not everyone on your team is going to get along. Our chaotic, high-pressure environment only makes poor relationships worse.

But troubled teams are paying a steep price for intragroup hostility. People avoid working together. They miss one another's input. They exclude one another from important decisions. They backbite. They bend other people's ears with their frustration and distract them from their priorities.

All in all, intragroup hostilities eat away at everyone's precious time and energy. And your organization, your staff, and your customers lose out.

You don't have to feel powerless in the face of disharmony. You don't have to settle for it. In your role as leader and coach, you can bring the disharmony out of the closet. You can acknowledge that you see it, and then you can prescribe a relationship-healing process to the conflicting parties. In fact, you can use your power to insist that they try it.

A Healing Approach

Ask the two people in conflict to meet or go to lunch and interview each other. Give them the following directives to resolve their issues:

Begin with a statement of *our positive intention*. Tell each other, "To use our energy optimally and produce the results the organization needs from us, it would be nice to reduce the strain between us and strengthen our relationship."

Then get better acquainted by asking each other some questions:

- How did you become involved in health care? What attracted you?
- As long as you've been in health care, what have you found to be most satisfying in your job? What are the high points?
- What have you found to be frustrating in your job and the field?
- What do you see as one important (big or small) achievement in your health care experience? And what was your specific role in it?
- In your job now, what do you find most satisfying?
- In your job now, what do you see as your greatest challenge?

Now ask about your relationship and perceptions of each other:

- From your perspective, what do you see as my strengths? What do you appreciate about me?
- From your perspective, what do I do or not do that frustrates you? What do you resent?
- What do you wish I would do that would make our relationship better?

Recapitulate by asking:

- How do you feel about this conversation? Any surprises?

Plan for the future:

- Given our goal to have a productive, constructive, and mutually respectful relationship, and given that, as leaders, we are role models for other leaders, what working agreements do we need that will keep us on track?
- How and when should we check in with each other to discuss our progress and needed course corrections?

Say thanks!

Taking Initiative

Yes, it takes nerve to suggest this process. And it takes nerve to do it. But you know how demoralizing it is for everyone when leaders are at odds—whether sparring for resources, power, or recognition. With members of your leadership team besieged with challenging work and ambitious goals, why not take the initiative to heal their relationships so you can leverage their strengths?

• • •

Additional Tools

Tool 1
PARTNER PROJECTS

Some of the relationships across department lines are so dysfunctional or non-existent that the two departments expend their precious energy pursuing work-arounds. They are unlikely to identify shared aspirations and work together to achieve them. They feel too drained from the bad blood between them. The managers involved lack "stretch" objectives that they own together. They have resigned themselves to coping with each other one day at a time.

If one manager is clearly less functional and effective than the other, you should be asking yourself why you're tolerating this. If both managers have redeeming strengths and you tolerate these rifts and allow workarounds, you are losing out on your managers' full capabilities and your organization has unused capacity.

If the two managers both add value individually, but not together, you need to change the dynamics between them. Force their hands by compelling them to work together to produce a valued result.

The approach:

- Call the managers together.
- Ask them to describe the interdependencies of their two departments.
- Assert that you want to see greater synergy and partnership between them.
- State the strategic priorities for your organization, and assign managers a project that advances one or more of those priorities.

Partner Project Instructions

Together, identify an initiative that can enhance one of our organization's strategic objectives—an initiative that, working together, you have the power to make happen.

- Share perceptions of the services that cut across your two departments' lines.
- Identify common ground in terms of improvement opportunities. Focus on one opportunity that you consider important.
- Pinpoint the goal(s).
- Define the approach.
- Implement it according to your plan.
- When you have succeeded, set a meeting with me (within two months).
  —Present to me your goal, approach, and accomplishments.
  —Each of you describe and promote the other person's (not your own) contributions to making this initiative happen.
  —Share what worked well in your collaboration and what you learned about each other in the process.
  —You cannot postpone this meeting. You've got to make the deadline. Make it happen!

After seven weeks, if you don't see a partner project meeting on your calendar, contact the twosome and demand it within the week.

The psychology of this tool: If necessary, force people to work together. If you can strong-arm them into a successful experience, they might find that they have been wrong in their perceptions of each other and may become unstuck. It's worth a try.

Tool 2
THE DANCE CARD FOR
STRENGTHENING RELATIONSHIPS

It's human nature to put troubled relationships on the back burner, going out of your way to avoid the person so you won't have to deal with him or her directly. The result: a stalemate. The troubled relationship continues to be troubled, or worse, it grows into an outright hostile relationship.

This tool takes courage. It involves creating a "dance card" for yourself—a dance card on which you place the names of the managers or physicians in your organization who give you grief. Make a commitment to yourself that you will set one appointment each month with one of these people and address your concerns directly.

Here's an example of such a dance card:

Dance Card for Strengthening Key Relationships

- January: Bill
- February: Ronnie
- March: Helena
- April: Mac

Follow this formula for setting up the meeting:

- State your positive intent: "Our departments are interdependent. We rely on each other. I would like a better relationship with you—a relationship that works for both of us and for our customers."
- Propose a time, place, and length of time for your appointment.
- Propose an agenda and invite the person to add and bring his or her agenda items, too.
- Repeat your positive intent.
- Thank the person for agreeing to talk with you.

Prepare for the meeting by using this worksheet:

I appreciate . . .	
I resent . . .	
I am asking of you . . .	

At the meeting:

- Show up.
- State specific appreciations and mean them.
- Be tactfully direct with your resentments and concerns.
- Invite the other person to do the same.
- See if you can reach agreements.
- Thank the person genuinely for working with you to strengthen your relationship.

Chapter 6

• • •

The Meeting Meter

Have staff members evaluate meetings
at their end so you can run
future meetings more efficiently.

Do the following comments sound familiar?

- "I'm swamped, and I eat up all my time in meetings!"
- "That meeting could have been an e-mail!"
- "I start the day with high hopes about what I'm going to get done, but my to-do list just grows. And on the way home, I feel drained, like I didn't accomplish anything."
- "If I didn't waste so much time in meetings, I could do my work."

Many people find their meetings so deadly, it's no wonder they often call an evaluation of them a "postmortem." One meeting after another consumes executives' precious time without yielding benefits.

What You're Paying

Let's look at the cost of just one meeting. Imagine a two-hour, seven-person executive team meeting, and assume an average hourly rate of $65 per hour per executive. That meeting costs $910.

Of course, the salary is not the only price you're paying. When you and your associates are in meetings, you are not advancing other priorities or coaching or managing your people. The piles in your in-basket and in-box are growing by the minute.

You are not meeting with customers or physicians. You are sequestered. You are not available to guide or support others. You are not available to take questions or calls.

Estimate the average hourly rate of the people in each of your meetings. Multiply this rate by the length of the meeting. Then, at the start of the meeting, post for all to see the cost of people's time. Add to it the cost of opportunities lost from being in the meeting and tasks not performed.

When you post the meeting's cost, people become both more conscious and self-conscious about time spent in meetings and their contributions. Also, if people think the group is frittering away its precious time, someone is more inclined to say, "We're wasting time, money, and opportunity by the minute!"

Using the Meeting Meter

When you're driving in your car and you hit a curb, you instinctively turn the wheel to straighten yourself out. Just as hitting the curb provides corrective feedback, so does the Meeting Meter. When you and your team use it to evaluate each of your meetings, the process prompts you to make quick, critical course corrections.

Have people complete the Meeting Meter at the meeting's end (see the figure on the next page). Whether you share results on the spot or collect and review them anonymously, you'll find the feedback informative.

The Meeting Meter

	Yes	No
1. We had a written agenda for this meeting.		
2. We addressed the important things first so we wouldn't run out of time for them.		
3. We had time limits associated with each item on the agenda.		
4. The agenda was circulated ahead of time so we could prepare.		
5. The meeting started on time.		
6. The purpose of the meeting was clear.		
7. A designated person took minutes so we could recall correctly the decisions and agreements.		
8. We stayed focused; we didn't meander.		
9. We kept to the agenda unless we decided as a group to depart from it for good reason.		
10. We used the time efficiently.		
11. Everyone had a chance to talk.		
12. The meeting ended on time.		
13. It's clear who's supposed to do what as a result of this meeting.		
14. This meeting involved dialogue. A written communication couldn't have taken its place.		
15. This meeting was necessary. More than one perspective was needed.		
16. This meeting was worth its price.		

Taking Notes

Yes, it's a pain to take notes. But if you want your meetings to go beyond talk and reap results, someone needs to do it. The simple format in the figure below does the trick.

With health care leaders feeling so utterly swamped, it is a matter of respect to make your meetings matter.

The Meeting Recap

Team Name:	Date:	
Recap Preparer:	Meeting Leader:	
Attendees:	Send Copies to:	
Agenda	Decisions/Agreements	
Assignments	Person Responsible	Deadline

• • •

Additional Tools

Tool 1
QUICK MEETING LIGHTENERS WITH A FOCUS

To make the most of your team meetings, start with a warm-up that breaks the ice while also focusing your team on the substance of the meeting. Here are a few examples.

Imagine you're going to be discussing accountability, rounding, or revenue-generating options. You can focus the warm-up on the topic, whatever it is.

The Limerick Warm-up

Instructions:

- Divide into groups of twos or threes.
- In your small group, develop a limerick on _____.
- Prepare to read it to the whole group. (You will have five minutes of prep time.)

To be a limerick, a verse must follow this format:

- It must have five lines.
- Lines one, two, and five have nine stressed syllables, and they rhyme.
- Lines three and four have five stressed syllables, and they also rhyme.

Limerick Examples
(from a meeting about accountability for service excellence)

Oh stop all that silly complaining.
My listening tolerance is waning.
Please get your act together
No matter what the weather.
Or I don't think you will be remaining.

We have many customers—needy
And we don't want our care to be seedy.
With high standards of service,
We won't have to feel nervous.
We'll be proud and successful indeedy.

Tool 2
THE HAIKU WARM-UP

Haiku is a Japanese poem with three lines and as many as seventeen syllables. Challenge your team in pairs to develop a haiku on the meeting topic of the day or on specific agenda items.

Example: Haiku Meeting Warmup

Haiku has three lines and a seventeen-syllable maximum (usually five syllables in line 1, seven syllables in line 2, and five syllables in line 3).

Meeting Agenda Item	Haiku Example
Financial health	Enough to pay bills. Not nearly enough to gloat. The right direction.
Key messages to our employees	People on the move. Accomplishing caringly. No easy feat. Thanks!
To grow or not to grow?	Priority load. Is there enough energy? Maybe we should breathe.

Worksheet for Haiku Warmup

Meeting Agenda Item	Your Haiku
1.	
2.	
3.	

Copyright ©2006 Wendy Leebov

Tool 3
THE FIVE NOTS

Divide your team into pairs. Have all of the dynamic duos brainstorm five ways to not do a successful job of something you're discussing on your agenda. Encourage humor and competition by bringing a booby prize or laugh meter.

The "Five Nots!" List: With your partner, spend five minutes creating a list of five nots.

How Not to (e.g., increase revenue, do rounds, strengthen relationships with medical staff)

1.

2.

3.

4.

5.

Tool 4
PROCESS FLAGS

Follow these steps to ensure healthy and productive meetings.

Preparation:

- Engage your team in establishing explicit ground rules for individual and group behavior during meetings.
- Post these permanently where people can easily refer to them during your meetings.
- Locate or make little yellow flags and put them in a basket on the conference table.

At each meeting:

- At the start, ask people to quickly reread the ground rules.
- Give each person a little yellow flag with the instruction, "Wave the flag if you think we're somehow off course in the meeting. It is the responsibility of every one of us to keep this meeting on course. When you wave the flag, you will get everyone's attention so you can make a process comment or suggestion."
- At the end of the meeting, ask people to take a minute to reflect and comment on the ground rules. Ask:
  —How did we do during this meeting?
  —What did we do well? How did we fall short?
  —In the next meeting, what should we do to make it better?

Chapter 7

• • •

E-mail Etiquette

*E-mail can save valuable time
and greatly improve efficiency, but misusing it
causes interpersonal problems that
drain everyone's energy and time.*

I'm a customer service fanatic. I believe that every one of us has customers, whether we serve patients or we serve the people who do. Our colleagues are also our customers, and they deserve considerate, respectful, direct communication, regardless of the medium. That includes e-mail.

While many of us glory in this miracle of modernization, the misuses and abuses of e-mail ruffle the feathers of customers and co-workers alike. Below I offer a list of e-mail dos and don'ts.

E-mail Dos

Limit the quantity and length of e-mails to the essentials. Lengthy e-mails can be confusing and can require clarification via further e-mails. One telephone call may save an afternoon of e-mail exchanges. Restrict your message to one screen or two at the most.

Consider the sensitivity of the issue. Sometimes, business is better done with customers or colleagues face to face or by phone. Resolve controversial issues and discuss sensitive subjects in person.

Think about nuance. Your friendly, joking tone may not be received in the same positive way you intended. Reread your e-mails before pushing "send" to make sure they won't create unintended negative consequences.

Send critical, time-sensitive information in a timely fashion. When a reply is urgent or information has to be handled immediately, place a telephone call or page.

Check your e-mail regularly. Reply even if you don't have an answer, acknowledge receipt, and explain your plan. For instance, "I'll have to think this through. I'll get back to you by end of day tomorrow." Print or otherwise mark those e-mails that you need to think about and handle later.

Develop an orderly filing system for those e-mail messages you wish to keep. Delete unwanted ones to conserve disk space.

Think about security and confidentiality. E-mails are as secure as a post-card message. Recognize that anyone along the chain of distribution may see what you have said and forward it to others.

If you need to send a sensitive message, use some form of encrypting (known only to you and the recipient), or use some other, more secure medium.

When you receive an e-mail from Frank and forward Frank's e-mail along with your comments to another person, ask yourself whether you're violating Frank's confidentiality by including Frank's e-mail in your outgoing message.

Remember that your e-mails are not private. In a business, the organization is permitted to authorize people to read your e-mail.

Respect the reader's time. Ensure that your message is clear so your recipient doesn't waste time trying to interpret your message.

Make the subject field of your e-mail message meaningful and descriptive. The subject "Oops, did it again!" will indeed get the receivers' attention, but it does not allow them to prioritize their work. Also, it makes it hard to file and find your e-mail if needed for the future.

Restrict yourself to one topic per message. Send multiple messages if you have multiple subjects, each with a description of the topic in the subject line.

When you respond to an e-mail, attach the original message to your response.

Encourage others to communicate with you by e-mail. Make sure you give them your correct e-mail address. Include it on your business card and letterhead. If you limit the times when you open your e-mail, adjust people's expectations about when you will read it.

Understand that the various laws relating to written communication apply to e-mail messages. These include laws relating to defamation, copyright, obscenity, fraudulent misrepresentation, freedom of information, and wrongful discrimination.

Remember that sending e-mail from your account is similar to sending a letter on your organization's letterhead. Don't say anything that could discredit or embarrass you, your colleagues, or the organization.

E-mail Don'ts

Snipping: Being curt; addressing an emotion-laden issue with a response that's all business.

Sniping: Copying your colleague's boss on an e-mail in which you reprimand or remind that colleague that something is overdue or underdone.

Dumping: Using the "send" button to get the problem off your back and on someone else's.

Distracting: Sending chain e-mails, fun Web finds, or jokes that consume others' valuable time and waste system resources.

Grumping: Fuming when it takes a while to get an answer, as if the person on the receiving end has nothing to do but sit there awaiting your message.

Pumping: Asking for information that you wouldn't have the nerve to ask for in person.

Clumping: Sending e-mail to a group of people, some of whom have no business receiving it.

SCREAMING: Using all caps for emphasis.

Broadcasting: Forwarding an e-mail meant for your eyes only.

Jumping: Giving an irritated, derisive response to an e-mail that touched your nerve.

Drowning: Sending an e-mail that goes on and on and on and on and leaves the poor readers frustrated and fuming as they search for your point and wonder if perhaps you don't have enough to do.

Misfiring: Responding mistakenly to the person who wrote the attachment, instead of to the person who sent it to you.

Freezing: Failing to acknowledge or respond in any way to an e-mail that asks for a response.

A Few Words about Voice Mail

Voice mail is hardly obsolete: Sometimes a computer isn't handy, or you want to explain something in your own voice. Voice mail contributes to efficient communication by allowing the caller to leave a detailed and specific message or explanation. By polishing your approach to voice mail, you can show that you care about both your own and the receiver's time.

Leave your name, the time and date of the call, the nature of the call, and your return phone number. This allows the person you're calling to respond to the specific issue or request or prepare a response to you. When you leave a "call me back" message without your number, you leave the listener with two tasks: calling you back and looking for your number.

Check your voice mail frequently (at least daily). Reach agreement with your team about the time frame for responding that you will all follow.

Use voice mail as a backup system. In customer service areas, all calls should be answered personally during business hours. On the rare occasion when this is impossible, voice mail offers the caller the option of leaving a message or dialing a backup number answered by a living, breathing human being. Make every effort to avoid situations in which the backup number also terminates in voice mail.

Adopt Guidelines as a Team

Why not work with your team to establish, publicize, and adhere to ground rules that reduce misuses and abuses of e-mail? Think of the time and emotional energy everyone will save and the relationship snags and misunderstandings that could be avoided. Also, if all leaders were role models of effective, constructive, considerate use of e-mail (and voice mail), others throughout the organization would follow suit.

The bottom line: Communication devices are for communicating. When people misuse them, the communication lapses and affronts end up draining individuals, the team, and the organization of its most precious resource—time.

• • •

Additional Tools

Tool 1
E-MAIL PROMPTS FOR ALIGNMENT AND CHANGE

A series of e-mails can be a powerful tool for executives to focus attention on the many actions managers need to take to implement planned change. How often have you heard:

- "Will this be another flash in the pan like other things we've done here?"
- "Will executives walk the talk?"

These are typical examples of skeptical statements about organizational change strategies, like initiatives designed to elevate patient and employee satisfaction. The process indeed must be long term, with persistent focus and tenacity.

Individuals or teams coordinating the nuts and bolts of your change strategy are in the best position to design a series of e-mails, or "e-mail prompts," so that their content and timing fit each strategy step. Ask the strategists to develop the e-mail series for you. Then edit it to your liking and style, and clarify who should push "send" for each e-mail and when.

Here are examples of e-mail prompts from one component of a service excellence strategy that focused on implementing *wow* performance of everyday greetings, handoffs, and goodbyes.

From: Administrator to Managers/Supervisors

Subject: Getting started with *wow* greetings

When I envision how our hospital will feel to our patients, families, and each other when we all do a *wow* job of greetings, I'm excited! Hopefully by now you have read through the timeline and are gearing up to start the Greetings Campaign with your team on (date).

Here are my suggestions about what to do now:

- Start role-modeling service excellence and especially great greetings.
- Read "Using Scripts for Patient Interactions" from this tool kit for ideas on scripting great greetings.
- Talk with your teams about attending an employee workshop. Address questions and concerns, and communicate your *personal* commitment.

- Decide when and how you will introduce staff to the greetings follow-up campaign, and discuss your strategy for engaging them in developing job-specific scripts.
- Give your team an overview of the campaigns; tell them about the upcoming greetings campaign.
- Thank and appreciate people whose performance is great.

As we move forward, don't hesitate to bolster this campaign with your own creative ideas. Also, please contact me with questions, concerns, insights, feedback, or stories at any point. I'm determined to do my part.

From: Executive to Managers/Supervisors

Subject: Update, please!

How did your team's greetings kickoff go? Will you please send me a quick e-mail to let me know?

From: Executive to Managers/Supervisors

Subject: Checking on *wow* greetings

I'm interested to know how your team members are responding to the idea and approach to scripting *wow* greetings tailored to their specific jobs. Please drop me a line to clue me in. Thanks.

From: Executive to Managers/Supervisors

Subject: Script examples, please

While I'm rounding, I'm happy to say that I'm feeling the warmth of people's greetings.

I would like to compile and circulate a few examples of job-specific scripts for *wow* greetings that your team has developed. Please send me a script that you think is a *wow* script, with a sentence telling me the position(s) that are employing it.

Thanks much!

From: Leader to Managers/Supervisors

Subject: Schedule script rehearsals

Now is the time to determine the best format for your team to rehearse your job-specific scripts. You and/or your stars can do this in meetings, by providing buddies or coaches or holding mini-practice sessions in small groups. Here are tools to spark your thinking about how you want to do this. (Attach tools.)

From: Manager to Staff

Subject: Let's recognize each other and celebrate

I have a pile of certificates, caught-in-the-act coupons, and telegrams on my desk. I invite you to take some, fill them out, and give them to specific team members you want to commend for implementing greetings in a *wow* way. Please help us recognize the individual effort and care that is going into this process!

From: Manager to Staff

Subject: Greetings check-up coming up

I want to let you know that we will soon begin distributing a greetings check-up to a few of our customers to invite feedback about our team's effectiveness with greetings. The forms will be in a box on the front desk . . . take a look!

From: Executive to Managers/Supervisors

Subject: Check-in on greetings

I want to know what improvements you've noticed in how your team members are greeting patients and other customers at this point. Please drop me a line to tell me your observations or share your questions and concerns.

From: Manager to Staff

Subject: *Wow* greetings practice

Would you benefit from a little one-on-one practice of wow greetings? I'll gladly make available a "buddy" to help people fine-tune and get more comfortable with great greetings. So please let me know if you're interested, and I'll arrange it.

From: Executive to All Staff

Subject: Patients are telling us . . .

Here are some comments we've received on our most recent greetings check-ups. All of our work providing *wow* greetings is starting to show results.

- Quote
- Quote
- Quote

See you at the party!

Tool 2
GOOD NETIZENSHIP

In a leadership meeting, uncover what might otherwise be unspoken frustrations within the team about one another's e-mail and Internet behavior.

1. Make an opening statement: "We are all pressed for time and appreciate other people respecting this fact. One thing that eats away at our time, creating avoidable frustration, is irritating e-mail from *each other*. Let's take a few minutes to check in on each other's pet peeves with e-mail, so we can respect these likes and dislikes and be more effective in communicating within our team."
2. Ask everyone to quickly fill out this netizenship meter (see next page).
3. Afterward, share results by reading one item at a time and asking people to show their rating by holding up the appropriate number of fingers.
4. Brainstorm other pet peeves related to e-mail or Internet behavior.
5. Invite the group to share these.
6. Pose the following questions: "Now what? What code of good netizenship do we want to follow for the sake of the team? What commitments can we make to each other about netiquette that will help to reduce people's frustrations, respect people's time, and ease our communication with each other?"
7. In closing, make these suggestions:
    *   When in doubt, ask your colleagues for guidance and feedback. Invite colleagues to state their preferences regarding net communication with you.
    *   Speak up if you are on the receiving end of a co-worker's netiquette violation.

The Netizenship Meter

On a scale from 1 to 5, with 1 being "I like it" and 5 being "Big pet peeve," complete this checklist.

	1 I like it	2	3	4	5 Big pet peeve
1. Someone who expects you to engage in instant messaging with them just because you appear to be online					
2. E-mails that don't make the subject clear in the subject line					
3. Receiving e-mails written in all CAPS (called screaming)					
4. Receiving cute items from the Web					
5. Seeing that someone who received an e-mail from you forwarded your e-mail to other people					
6. Long e-mails—going on and on without getting to the point					
7. Being confronted through an e-mail rather than in a conversation					
8. Receiving no response at all when you ask a question via e-mail, not even "I got your question and I'll need to think about it, and I'll get back to you tomorrow."					
Other					
Other					

Chapter 8

• • •

Starts with Me

Give employees permission and tools
to stop problem behavior among colleagues
as soon as it starts.

"If it is to be, it starts with me." Wouldn't it be great if every person on our health care teams approached patient satisfaction with this attitude?

It's a mind-bending challenge to hold employees accountable for service standards—for performing consistently in ways that foster high levels of patient and family satisfaction. Here are just a few of the reasons managers give for insufficient accountability.

Why Accountability Is So Hard

"I'm not there to see. And if I am, they behave better while I'm watching. Also, I might see some people but miss others, and I don't want to be accused of being unfair."

"It's the customer's word against the employee's. There's no way to know the truth."

"If I confront the employee, they and their co-workers might resent it. Then they'll act even worse. I can't afford to lose the respect of my team."

"With the staffing shortage, I can't afford to alienate anyone. A warm body is better than nobody."

"It's an endless, tedious process, and I don't have time. You have to go through hoops because of human resources policies."

Health care executives can present arguments to counter these excuses. They can also harangue managers to stop rationalizing and boldly confront staff performance problems for the sake of patients and the team. That is important, but it hasn't proven to be enough.

Many managers at all levels cringe at the thought of what they view as heavy-handed accountability tactics. And people at all levels who are committed to service excellence (that's the majority) feel frustrated when their co-workers behave inappropriately with patients and customers and suffer no consequences.

How about taking an approach to accountability that doesn't fall on managers' shoulders alone? How about putting a tool and process into the hands of all employees, so that when they see problem behavior and want to nip it in the bud, they have permission and an agreed-upon way to do it?

The Peer Feedback Approach to Accountability

In my experience, great employees get frustrated with managers who fail to hold people accountable. And when it comes to customer service, we all know that the great people end up with twice the work because customers and co-workers alike seek them out, making end runs around the more frustrating staff members.

Develop and promote a co-worker feedback process. Engage your team in committing to an agreed-upon method everyone can use to nip problems in the bud, whether they know the co-worker or not. This will help alleviate a sense of powerlessness and discouragement among the many people who want to feel proud of their own and others' behavior.

Keys to Shared Responsibility for Accountability

1. **Commitment:** Agree that responsibility for accountability starts with every member of the team.
2. **Common language:** Agree on language and signals everyone can use when they see both negative and exemplary behavior on the part of others who do not report to them, others they might not even know. Steep managers in skill building and practice so they can be effective models and coaches of both negative and positive feedback.

3. **Communication and spread:** Spread the goal, the expectation, and the language throughout the organization.

4. **Team gain sharing:** By tying compensation to overall patient satisfaction, further encourage people to speak with each other to achieve impressive performance across levels and department lines.

Diagnose problems and missed opportunities. The following worksheet can help you review current practices and bring to the surface any issues and challenges.

The situation: Who behaves inappropriately?	Example of uncaring behavior or missed opportunity for caring behavior:	What do managers do now when they see it?	What do you think managers should do when they see it?	What do you wish staff would do when they see it?
1. Your own employee				
2. Another manager				
3. An employee who reports to another manager				
4. An administrator				
5. A physician				
6. An employee widely known to be rude or having a bad attitude and who continues to act that way. This person's manager appears to be doing nothing about it. It really bothers you.				

Develop shorthand signals. It's very helpful to agree on language short-hand everyone can use to make it easier to speak up.

- Negative feedback shorthand: Develop a constructive, caring signal people can use in an "oops" situation to alert another person to something they're doing that is uncaring or misses an opportunity to be caring. This might be a gesture, such as raising an arm, stretching, or scratching an itchy nose; or it might be words, such as "I see an opportunity" or "bing." Also agree on a caring opening line that frames specific negative feedback positively. For example: "I know you care. So here's a bit of feedback for you. . . ."
- Positive regard shorthand: Agree on a shorthand people can use to call a co-worker's attention to something very positive that they did, such as "ta-daah" or "kudos." Also, agree on an opening line that frames the appreciation well. For example: "I saw you _____ and I'm impressed."

The worksheet below can guide creative brainstorming of possible language signals people can use to give caring feedback to others.

Let's Design Shorthand for Caring Feedback

Feedback Type	Example of Shorthand/Signal	Your Ideas Go Here
Positive	"WOW!" "Impressive!" "Kudos to you!"	
Negative	"Oops" "Star situation" "Notice"	

Develop a language model. In many cases, the shorthand will be all that people need to use because the use of the shorthand signal will make co-workers realize immediately what they did. In other cases, they might not realize the problem. So the feedback giver will need to explain further. Agree on a language model for caring feedback—a model that prompts people to describe behavior and consequences if the person they're addressing doesn't instantly realize what he or she did or didn't do.

Great Language Model for Peer Feedback

Feedback Elements	Your Ideas Go Here
1. Opening: "I know you care. So I think you'll want to know . . ." "I noticed a missed opportunity . . ."	
2. Describe behavior: "I saw/heard . . ."	
3. Consequences (for me, patients, families, team, organization):	
4. Pinch of empathy: "Now I realize . . ."	
5. Suggestion or request: "I think you could show more empathy by. . . . I'm asking you to _____ in the future."	

Practice Makes Proficient

Because giving feedback, especially peer feedback, tends to fall outside people's comfort zones, it's essential to provide practice to make giving feedback easier. Here's a worksheet that can be a template for language practice in work teams.

Feedback Practice

Comment or Action	Feedback: What can you say to the person to caringly confront his or her behavior?
1. "Look, we're really busy. We've had several people call out, and we don't have enough staff."	
2. While taking a patient down a hallway, the employee stops to talk with a friend, taking focus away from the patient.	
3. To a request for help, employee responds, "That's not my job."	
4. "Oh no! Another patient!"	
5. Another manager's employee is rude to a patient.	
6. "That department is always late!"	
7. In the elevator, staff talk about a patient (with strangers present).	
8. Executive walks past employees without acknowledging them in any way.	
9. "Look, you're not our only patient!"	
10. Doctor treats an employee with disrespect.	

You can use a similar template to engage people in practicing positive feedback as well.

Yes, a Culture Change

Let's face it: Many traditional approaches to accountability are cumbersome, negative, and avoided. And the burden on managers to have eyes and ears in the back of their heads is unrealistic. It's time to empower all the wonderful people on our teams to help—by giving them the tools, coaching, role modeling, and encouragement they need—so that they too will egg their co-workers on to achieve impressive service and patient satisfaction.

• • •

Additional Tools

Tool 1
POEM ON ACCOUNTABILITY

As leader, I AM RESPONSIBLE
for my team's performance.
I am.

When my team members are great,
We all win.
Patients and all.

If my team is not GREAT,
I've stopped short.
I have more to do.

If I allow weak links,
I'm saying,
"This is good enough."

My team's performance
reflects on me.
I'm leading the way.

Copyright ©2006 Wendy Leebov

Tool 2
BASIC CIVILITY SELF-ASSESSMENT

To achieve *great* service, we as leaders must create a *culture of accountability.*

- As individuals, we must take personal responsibility for displaying attitudes and behavior that advance our mission and values.
- As leaders, we must hold our teams and each other accountable for meeting high standards consistently.
- It starts with *basic civility.* To what extent do you treat basic civility unflinchingly as a non-negotiable job requirement?

Civility Self-Assessment

Ask Yourself	Yes	No
1. Do I believe that civility is possible today despite the pressures my team and I are facing?		
2. Do I screen job candidates for civility?		
3. Do I coach or arrange coaching for employees who are marginal in their civility?		
4. Do I engage my team in identifying specific civility behavior that will *impress* customers?		
5. Is my staff utterly clear that civility is really important to me?		
6. Do I believe that negative people should be confronted when they are interfering with patient and/or co-worker satisfaction?		
7. Do I often communicate my commitment to impressive civility?		
8. Do I exemplify *caring* in my interactions with patients and staff?		
9. Do I set ambitious performance expectations to those who report to me?		
10. Do I monitor employee performance regularly?		
11. Do I frequently appreciate and thank people who show warmth, care, and concern in their interactions with patients and each other?		

To be fully effective at holding yourself and others accountable for civility, you should say "yes" to all of these questions. When you answered "no," that means this behavior on your part is an improvement opportunity.

Tool 3
SERVICE EXCELLENCE—
DO I PRACTICE WHAT I PREACH?

- We're in a fishbowl. All eyes are checking to see if we're practicing what we preach.
- As leaders, we must be the change we want to create! We need to use our power and visibility to be exemplary role models of service excellence. Consider your effectiveness as service excellence role model in fundamental everyday situations: great greetings, handoffs, goodbyes, and interdepartmental/co-worker relationships.

Strength	Room for Improvement	Greetings
		I greet people I know and people I don't know in a welcoming fashion.
		I greet every person I pass when I'm in public areas.
		When someone comes to my office, I give a warm welcome before delving into the business at hand.
		I give my staff feedback on their greeting performance.
		I compliment people on their greeting style when I think it's really effective.
Strength	Room for Improvement	Handoffs
		I pay attention to the transitions and follow-through that I do.
		When delegating tasks, I do so in a *great* way.
		I give my staff feedback on their handoff performance.
		I compliment people on their handoff style when I think it's very effective.

(Continued on next page)

Strength	Room for Improvement	Goodbyes
		I say a gracious goodbye to people I know and people I don't know.
		I say goodbye to people I pass as I leave the building or as I see them leaving.
		When someone leaves my office, I wish him or her a warm and appreciative goodbye.
		I give my staff feedback on their goodbye performance.
		I compliment my staff members on their goodbye style when I think it's effective.

Strength	Room for Improvement	Interdepartmental/Co-worker Relationships
		I pitch in. I extend a helping hand.
		I communicate directly when I have a concern.
		I promote my colleagues. I build customer confidence in our organization's whole team, not just my staff.
		I treat my employees with consideration and respect.
		I treat people in other departments with consideration and respect.
		I am responsive to people's phone calls and requests.
		I keep promises and deadlines. I follow through.
		I express appreciation and thanks to my team.
		I express appreciation and thanks to colleagues in other departments.
		I actively encourage my team to build cooperative relationships across department lines.

My greatest strengths as service excellence role model are _____.

Improvement opportunities I see for myself are _____.

Chapter 9

● ● ●

Healthy Respect

*An acknowledgment of the essential
dignity of all, healthy respect can
transform a contentious environment
into a healing one.*

There is not nearly enough healthy respect flowing through health care organizations. This fact adversely affects not only the people who work for us but also the people we serve.

The pecking order makes a lot of wonderful, contributing people feel inferior. The people on the downside too often feel discounted and invisible. It's hard to do your best under those conditions.

I donned a transporter uniform a few weeks ago and, as a transport trainee, shadowed a transporter in a big hospital. I wanted to see firsthand the interactions between transporters and patients so I could identify the customer service challenges in the transporter role and why transporters so often get a bad rap. As it turns out, I was very impressed with transporter interactions with patients and families. It was the interactions between transporters and nurses that took me aback.

I was glad to hear that partnerships between nursing and transport work extremely well on some units: there are no complaints on either side, and they respect one another. In other instances, I heard two starkly different viewpoints.

Nurse Perspective	Transporter Perspective
"Those transporters are always on the phone. And we have to wait for patient pickups."	"Don't they know that our dispatch system is a phone system?"
"You always see transporters walking together. How many transporters does it take to change a light bulb?"	"Don't they know that many patients require two transporters? We help each other. Also, we spend all day walking hallways. Of course, we're going to run into each other."
"Those transporters refuse to wait when the patient isn't ready. And it's not our fault when the patient isn't ready. There might be family there, or they might need to go to the bathroom, or maybe they're finishing their meal."	"They should get the patient ready when they call. When we get there and the patient isn't ready, we can only wait five minutes because of the other calls into the system. We're responsible for a certain number of calls an hour. We can't hang around waiting."
"Don't transporters realize that it isn't my fault when an order is canceled and it turns out that they made the trip for nothing?"	"Over half of our transport requests turn out to be cancelations or reschedulings. And often, no one from the floor calls to cancel even when he or she could cancel in plenty of time. Do you realize how much faster our service would be if we weren't spending more than half the day on false starts?"

Each party is looking at the facts of the matter through a different lens. Each party is feeling oppressed by the other.

Promoting Interdepartmental Respect: Seven Tools

Your management team can break down walls and build trusting relationships across departmental, cultural, positional, and authority lines. Please consider employing the following seven tools:

1. The road show—myth-dispelling communication
2. "Let's make a deal"—ground rules for interdepartmental partnerships
3. Scripting for difficult situations

4. Breaking down walls between people
5. Breaking down walls between departments
6. "Mirror, mirror on the wall"—the executive self-check
7. Positive regard

Tool 1: The Road Show—Myth-Dispelling Communication

With planned communication exercises, you can dispel the myths that each group has about the other.

Every month, feature one support department. The department seeking bridge building puts on a road show, starting with a true-false quiz on the department for managers. The road show presenter then addresses the facts and myths, providing managers with a fact sheet that will make it easy to dispel myths and build understanding within their team.

Road Show to Build Interdepartmental Bridges: Agenda

- Give a quiz on how transportation services works.
- State the facts (dispel the myths).
- Look at the performance indicators.
- Evaluate how transportation services has been performing on these indicators. List accomplishments.
- Describe a patient care team that exemplifies cooperation, and spell out the elements of that cooperation.
- Identify the challenges, barriers, and frustrations that interfere with the support department's effectiveness and job satisfaction.
- State your commitment to providing impressive service.
- Assert the need to work in partnership across department lines:
  —Let the support department share its plan to strengthen interdepartmental relationships.
  —From the point of view of the support department, show how clinical partners can do their part to help the support department provide its services.

Clinical departments should get a turn at the road show as well, because bridge building and understanding must be a two-way street.

Tool 2: "Let's Make a Deal"

If you have a notorious conflict between one or more patient care units and a particular support service, hold a meeting between the support service and the clinical service. Challenge the group to develop ground rules for co-worker relationships.

Ground Rules for Interdepartmental Partnerships

> - Work as effective partners to provide the patient with an excellent transportation experience.
> - Treat staff in other departments with respect, courtesy, and professionalism.
> - Support people in other departments. Make them look good in the eyes of the patient even when you might be frustrated with them behind the scenes.
> - In conflict situations, be professional even if others are not. Maintain your dignity and pride.
> - Communicate from your heart. Acknowledge people's feelings without judging.
> - Apologize when someone has been inconvenienced no matter whose fault it is. Use the *blameless apology*. Don't take the blame, and don't blame others.
> - When you need to hold your ground, hold your ground caringly.
> - When you have a concern, speak to the person directly instead of bad-mouthing them to others. Take the high road.

Then ask, "What issues do we need to address to live these ground rules with each other day after day?" Form a bridge team of representatives from both services to reach understandings. Culminate with a written service contract that bridge-team members present to their colleagues with a personal commitment and optimism.

Tool 3: Scripting for Difficult Situations

Especially in the face of status differences, many employees talk about reluctance to confront disrespectful treatment. What too often happens is covert, not overt, thus festering friction between those involved.

I don't think leaders should advise their employees to absorb and not react to disrespectful treatment from co-workers, whether a nurse, administrator, doctor, or co-worker in their own department. Allowing and absorbing disrespectful treatment makes people sick, and it makes teams sick. Devote training to help staff employ direct, tactful language—without defensiveness—in handling repeatedly ugly interactions.

Difficult-Situation Scripts for Transporters

	Tragic Words: Statements that Make Matters Worse	Magic Words: A More Caring Alternative
The caregiver says, "Where the hell have you been!?"	"Hold your horses. I've been working my tail off, just like you. And anyway, the call just came in to Transport 17 minutes ago."	"You sound really frustrated. I'm sorry about the delay. Now I'm here and I want to help."
You arrive at a unit to pick up a patient. The nurse looks surprised and says, "Oh, I thought you knew. The patient doesn't feel well, so she's not going." No one called to cancel.	"I wish you had called to cancel. You are wasting our time. How in the world would we know it was canceled? You think we read minds?"	"I realize this sometimes happens without advance notice. I would really appreciate your calling next time as soon as possible to cancel the transport order, so we can use our time more wisely. Thanks."
You arrive on a unit and can't find the nurse for instructions. You wait five minutes and leave. When you return, the nurse says, "So, you came and left without taking the patient! You should have waited."	"Do you think you're the only person who calls Transport? You think I'm supposed to sit and wait and waste my time while you get the patient ready, which you should have done before I got here?"	"I'm sorry about the delay for the patient. And I want to make your work easier, not harder. The fact is, I looked for you for five minutes, and when no one could find you or give me instructions about the patient, I left to take another patient. Now I'm here and I want to help."

Source: From the "Dealing with Difficult-for-Me People" Tool Kit, ©2006 Wendy Leebov.

Imagine a world in which warring parties talk to each other in a respectful way.

Tool 4: Breaking Down Walls between People

Help people get to know each other. Try this in staff meetings or an employee forum: Count off so you end up with diverse groups of six people each. Within these groups, have people pair up and interview each other, taking a few notes for later recall.

Mutual Interview

---

1. What do you actually do in your job here? What is a typical day?
2. What do you like best about your job?
3. What is frustrating about your job?
4. What do you enjoy doing outside of work?
5. What's something about you that you think others might be surprised to know?
6. Brag. What do you feel really good at within your job?

After people have had a chance to interview each other, give everyone a pair of operating room booties. Ask them to write their name on their booties and to give them to their partner, who then puts them on.

Reconvene the circles of six, and have each person talk from the point of view of the person he or she interviewed. They are thereby "walking in their partner's shoes," talking as their partner about themselves and their job.

Afterward, ask the whole group, "What impressed you?" You will hear people's newfound appreciation for each other.

Tool 5: Breaking Down Walls between Departments

Randomly pair up departments or services with one another. Each department or service is asked to get to know their partner department using any of a variety of suggested methods (e.g., visits, interviews, observations, shadowing). They need to learn what the department actually does. Who comprises their team? What special contributions do people make to the organization? What gives them pride in their work, and so on?

Then ask them to prepare a wonderful way to recognize and appreciate this other department (providing a small budget will help). In some organizations, these recognition events are held at a retreat. In others, the presentations are between the two involved departments only.

You can also encourage bulletin board displays or fact sheets to share findings with wider audiences. Every quarter, you can change pairings and build additional bridges.

Tool 6: "Mirror, Mirror on the Wall"

It's going to be hard to make any of the ideas above work if members of the leadership team don't demonstrate respect to all people. Take a quick look in the mirror.

Respect: Executive Self-Check

	Yes	No
1. Do I acknowledge all people as I pass in the halls and elevators, whether I know them or not?		
2. Do I attend events that celebrate teams, cultural differences, and departments?		
3. Do I spend time shadowing people in departments that partner with mine, just so I can appreciate what they do and the challenges they face every day?		
4. Do I say thanks when I hear or observe that people are working hard or working well?		
5. Do I send thank-you notes to people who might be surprised that I know or notice them?		
6. Do I use my leadership position to intervene when members of the organization are treating employees with disrespect?		
7. Do I call people what they prefer to be called instead of taking liberties with their names?		
8. Do I require all managers to act in a respectful manner toward employees, or else?		
9. Do I make a special effort to hire and promote people different from myself so I can have a team with diverse capabilities and styles that complement, but do not duplicate, one another's skills?		

If you answered any of these questions with a "no," you've identified an opportunity to build bridges through your own example.

Tool 7: Positive Regard

How about focusing on the positive? How about celebrating the nourishing, respectful relationships with people in other departments? Imagine the support service team identifying other units or departments with whom they have respectful, constructive team relationships. And imagine support services giving quarterly teamwork awards to those teams at a hoopla event. Those teams receiving the awards will likely feel appreciated; those not receiving the awards will hopefully be keenly aware of that fact.

Going against the Grain

You might be thinking, "But pecking orders are a fact of life!" Perhaps so. Still, you have the power to minimize their destructiveness and, by so doing, liberate people's energies and spirits.

We are in an industry composed of caring people motivated to do good in society and make a personal difference to other people. When we expressly show and build respect for each other, regardless of status, we create an organization that works for everyone.

● ● ●

Additional Tools

Tool 1
USE OF INTERPERSONAL INFLUENCE
IN A CONFLICT SITUATION

Sometimes in a conflict situation, frustrated managers get into a power play. A power play tends to make matters worse. An alternative to a power play or "payback" mentality is use of personal influence.

Influence is the ability to win people's cooperation or consent to use their energy, power, or resources on something important to you. Influence is a powerful tool because there's so little we can make happen in organizations by ourselves. And often, we don't have the position power or authority over others that allows us to demand what we want. So we need to influence others to go in the direction we want.

Suggested Steps

1. Set your goal on fostering a positive relationship, not "winning."
2. Seek solid information about what took place. Investigate and get the facts. Check your assumptions.

3. Find out what the other person wants.
4. Ask for what you want.
5. Negotiate. Talk, get clear with each other, and see if you can reach a mutually satisfying agreement.
6. If you can't reach agreement:
    a. Ask why.
    b. Explain what's important to you.
    c. Consider other options that would also satisfy you. Get creative.
    d. Ask what the person would want of you in order to go in the direction you want.
    e. If you can't reach agreement, tell the person frankly the consequences.
7. Persevere. Work at it. Show the strength of your commitment.
8. Ask for support from colleagues or friends, since these situations can be emotionally draining.

Tool 2
WHEN EXECUTIVES ARE AT ODDS—THE THREESOME MEETING

When executives are at odds with each other over time, courageous intervention is necessary in order to curb the steep price your organization will pay otherwise. Convene the parties who are at odds, and provide the agenda for their discussion. Urge them to persist in their discussions until they have identified and agreed upon an action plan for a relationship breakthrough. Here's a sample agenda for such a discussion among three warring executives:

1. Set ground rules—for example, only talk about issues that affect the team.
2. Identify the business value of collaboration among the three of you:
    - Look at the consequences of collaborating versus not collaborating.
    - Identify examples of prices paid already. Any lost business? Potential business slowed down? Missed opportunities? Embarrassments, perceptions by customers or colleagues, current suspicions about current projects/explorations?
3. Share to gain increased interpersonal understanding:
    - How/when I feel misunderstood . . .
    - I collaborate effectively when . . .
    - I don't collaborate effectively when . . .
    - To me, collaboration means . . .
    - I get suspicious when . . .
    - I get angry/resentful when . . .

4. Determine what has gone on that has gotten in the way of truly effective, rapid collaboration.

5. Work on the issues identified.

6. What agreements can the three of us make so we convey a united front?

7. How can we show this united front to our entire leadership team? In gestures? In language? In visible collaboration?

8. How should we follow up this discussion to make sure we're on course and to discuss issues and concerns before they again lead to rifts?

Tool 3
RESPECT DOS AND DON'TS

Discuss these with your team and see if you can agree on and commit to a set of ground rules for co-worker relationships.

How do strain and disrespect show?

- Backbiting ("Did you hear about Alice?")
- Friendly fire ("Where were *you*?")
- Cracks about other departments to patients and families ("They always do that.")
- It's-not-my-job mentality, or reluctance to help each other out ("I'm too busy. Ask someone else.")
- Workarounds ("I know it's their job, but they're impossible, and I can't deal with them.")

Actions that Show Respect

- Wipe out any thought that your job is more important than other people's. Every person's contribution matters to the effectiveness of the whole.
- Build up other people. Appeal to their strengths. Don't engage in bad-mouthing. Just don't.
- Nip disrespect in the bud. Speak up caringly when you feel disrespected: "I want to work well with you. When you do that, it makes it hard for me."
- *Show* your appreciation and respect.
  —Thank co-workers.
  —Express your appreciation.
  —Compliment them in front of patients and families.
- Help each other. Make each others' work and life easier.

Chapter 10

• • •

The Management Coach

Leaders who effectively develop their managers enhance the organization, improve their own performance, and ease their burden.

It's critically important to develop the managers who report to you. Their contributions propel your organization forward, reflect on your performance, and make your life more manageable.

All your managers—from top performers to low performers—need development. When your top performers keep learning and growing, they are more likely to stay. Middle performers will appreciate your investment and receive guidance to help them become more effective. Coaching lower performers will allow you to see their capabilities up close as well as give them solid support and a chance to improve. You'll also have a better idea about who is a keeper.

Ten Tips for Developing Your Managers

1. **Share the big picture.** Make it clear where your organization is going. This will let your managers lead better. It will also be easier to let go of control, because you can trust that you're all on the same page.

2. **Coach, delegate, and empower.** Don't overdirect or dump. After ensuring that everyone's in alignment, entrust and guide.

3. **Encourage an "experimenter" mind-set.** Your organization is served better by a supportive "live and learn" attitude than a judgmental "success or failure" approach. Urge managers to take calculated risks, reflect on the process and outcomes, and learn from

the experience. If you don't actively encourage risk taking—albeit calculated risk taking—managers might be stuck in the status quo because they're afraid to fail.

4. **Define active learning as a necessity. Insist on active learning as a core competency.** Evaluate managers on the *active learning* competency in every performance review.

5. **Show.** Don't just tell. Be a role model of the leadership competencies you want. Demonstrate the mind-set and skills required for change leadership. Pursue learning opportunities so you can show managers the way.

6. **Tune in to each manager as an individual.** Hold conversations with them to learn what makes them tick. Then match your coaching to their needs, styles, and preferences. Engage them in shaping their own development process.

7. **Provide diverse learning opportunities.** Support different approaches: buddies, mentors, action learning projects, discussions of case scenarios in staff meetings, peer presentations, reading, and training. Insist on the destination, but allow for and support different paths.

8. **Hold courageous conversations with individuals and your team.** Give direct, constructive feedback. Express your frustrations. Confront behavior and resistance that impede progress and change.

9. **Come to terms with the fact that learning takes time.** Invest the hours in coaching your managers now, and you'll enhance your organization's capabilities, saving time later. Don't begrudge managers who pursue job-related learning opportunities within work time.

10. **Realize that you can't do it all.** Understand that only by fully deploying all leaders will you make your life more manageable.

Great Conversations to Help Your Managers Learn

Great coaches understand that before they can help someone develop, they need to establish a relationship. The more information you have about how your people like to be supported, the easier it will be for you to build on their strengths and bolster their weaknesses.

Get to know your managers as individuals so you can more effectively support them. Use any of the following conversations to focus your discussions. You can even include these as five- or ten-minute components of your regular meetings with individuals. It's amazing how much you can learn in five minutes if you listen and use a focused set of questions. As well as you know your direct reports, you'll learn a lot more and gain an even better sense of how you can coach constructively. Also, your team will feel your care and intent to support them.

Find Out about Their Strengths and Motivations

This conversation will help you delegate appropriate projects to managers and benefit from their strengths.

Talents: What are the personal skills and assets that you bring to this job? What do you do well and want to build on?

Passion: What do you care about in or out of work? What gets you excited? What are you eager to learn more about?

Experience: What have you done or experienced in the past that could help our team or group? What life experience do you have that you know could be valuable?

Challenges: What are some opportunities you would like to explore? Are there areas you want to work on or develop?

Future: If there were no obstacles, nothing in your way, what would you like to be doing in five years? What would you like to do in the year ahead within this job to help move in that direction?

Find Out about Perceptions of Upcoming Challenges

When you know more about your managers' thoughts, feelings, and concerns regarding what's ahead for them, you'll know better how to focus your support.

- Tell me how you feel about your management challenges at this point.

- What do you like most about the challenges in your job?

- Is there anything about the challenges ahead that concerns you?

- How will the changes be good for you?

- How might the challenges not be good for you?

- What do you find you are well equipped to do to make the changes happen? What do you feel especially good at?

- What do you feel you're not so good at? What would you like to be able to do better?

- How can I help you lead the changes ahead?

Help Your Managers Savor Their Successes

In today's environment with overload and multiple priorities, it's not unusual for people to focus on what hasn't been accomplished yet.

Ask the individual to think about a recent success: "There are times in our careers when we feel really good about what we're contributing. Think about a time when you felt you were at your best. This could involve an experience with a customer or a co-worker or a project or goal. The key is that you felt successful in that situation."

Probe for the whole story of this success. Ask:

- What was the situation?
- What did you do?
- What did you think about it?
- What were your feelings then?
- What was the outcome?
- How did you feel about yourself and your work as a result of this experience?
- What is it about you that you think contributed to your success?
- What support or wise counsel did you find helpful in the process?
- How is this situation like or unlike other situations at work?
- What can I do to help you have more successful experiences in this job?

Thank them for sharing this with you, mentioning specifically a couple of highlights that particularly impressed you.

Find Out about Communication Preferences

This information helps you consider ways you can tailor your communications and expectations to the individual's preferred modes of operating.

Meetings: How often do you like to meet when you are working on a project?

Communication: How do you prefer to be communicated with? Through e-mail, weekly face-to-face meetings, phone calls, or a combination?

Status reporting: I would like you to keep me up to date on how you're doing and where you are in relation to the timeline we've established. How would you prefer to do that?

Feedback: How do you like to receive feedback? With a written note, in person, with a written summary before meeting face to face? And how often?

Autonomy: How much autonomy or independence do you prefer when you are working on a project?

Set Managers Up for Success with Specific Projects

Create the conditions, clarity, and expectations that make managers more likely to succeed and you more willing to let go of control. This tool helps anticipate and remove roadblocks.

Ask: What do you think might get in your way or make this effort difficult for you?

Then dig for specifics by posing these possible roadblocks:

- Unclear goals and guidelines
- Red tape
- Not enough time
- Lack of cooperation from others
- Insufficient access to you for help and support
- All criticism, no praise or appreciation

Listen to the manager's concerns and address them early on.

Coaching for Specific Projects

Use the following model to plan ahead for coaching interactions. Also, take this model with you into a coaching session to remind you of the steps in a constructive, respectful approach.

Process Step	Why This Step Is Important
Describe the goal and why it is important.	People need to see the big picture.
Invite the manager's point of view on both the goal and performance.	People need to feel heard and validated. There may be different sides to the issue.
Invite the manager to generate ideas and solutions.	People need to be part of the solution.
Respect, acknowledge, and build on the manager's ideas.	People need you to support their ideas and guide them in new ways.
Summarize and agree on a plan.	Both of you need a shared vision to avoid misunderstanding.
Work together to identify responsibilities and timelines; keep the maximum responsibility with the manager.	People need to be clear on their commitments and responsibilities.
Build the manager's confidence and self-esteem all the while.	People need to know you have faith in their abilities.

Addressing the Importance of Coaching

Because all executives and managers should be coaching their direct reports or others who they view as promising for succession planning, devote a management team meeting to meaningful coaching.

Leader Meeting: Coaching Is Critical!

Divide people into pairs. Instruct people to think of a significant coach in their life, someone who really helped them perform at a higher level. Ask them to tell their partner about this person and explain the circumstances.

Partners should ask these questions of each other:

- What did this person do to bring out the best in you?
- What did this person do or say to help you feel good about yourself and your abilities?
- What were the most important lessons you learned from this person?
- How can you apply what you learned from this person to your coaching approach with your team?

Finally, Thinking Like a Coach

To be an effective coach, you have to believe in coaching. When you catch yourself thinking thoughts that *discourage* you from empowering team members, replace them with thoughts that *encourage* you to coach and empower.

Leaders with a "directing" style often think these thoughts:	Consider these thoughts instead:
"Coaching will eat away at my precious time."	By coaching, you build capability that you can deploy toward your objectives.
"If I coach people to do the work, I'll lose control."	By coaching, you learn about what each individual can do. And they learn your agenda, so they can make decisions in alignment with it.
"If I give managers greater responsibility, they'll make mistakes, and I'll be blamed. The buck stops here."	By coaching instead of "dumping" work on people without guidance, you minimize the risks. If you don't give people more responsibility, they will remain stuck. More and more and more of the work will rest on you.
"Most people just want me to tell them what to do."	That may be true of some. But there is far too much for you to do than watch over each person's shoulder to give them frequent direction. Your life will be manageable only if you help them learn to think and function with some level of independence.
"If I teach my staff to do the work too well, I won't be needed anymore."	Every success by managers you supervise is your success. And if you coach and develop people, there will be many more of them.
"These people don't have what it takes."	Are you sure? First, give them ample, specific feedback. Clarify the improvements you expect. If the person doesn't then change, develop, or get needed help, there is a mismatch between that person's skills and the organization's needs. You need to surround yourself with people who can add value. Cut the cord.

It's All about Leverage

By taking an active role in developing your management team, you expand and leverage their strengths and yours. Customers, staff, and the organization all benefit.

● ● ●

Additional Tools

Tool 1
COMMUNICATION TIPS FOR EFFECTIVE COACHING

Set up the coaching relationship so that your employee can succeed and you can gain trust in them and their work. Your up-front investment will pay off in results, optimal performance, and a strong relationship with the employee. The following are communication tips for effective coaching:

- Ask questions: Help staff open up by asking open-ended, not yes-no questions. Talk less and question more.
- Don't judge: People shut down when they feel criticized or labeled. Make sure you state your feedback and observations constructively.
- Listen carefully: Try to absorb the meaning behind the words. Don't make assumptions. Ask people to explain so you are sure you understand. "Tell me more," is a nonthreatening way to get people to elaborate.
- Maintain an open mind: There are usually several ways to achieve a goal. Suspend disbelief and try to understand the employee's approach if it differs from yours. Give people space to experiment.
- Show support: Praise and build on their ideas. "Yes!" and "Good idea!" encourage people to continue the dialogue.
- Focus on the person: Talk about yourself and your experiences sparingly. You won't develop others by talking about yourself.
- Avoid comparisons: Use examples carefully. People don't like to be compared with other people. Watch saying, "When Mary and her group did this. . . ."
- Slow down: People won't open up when they feel rushed. Most people need time to assemble and express their thoughts, feelings, and ideas.
- Eliminate distractions: Your employees will not feel valued if you are distracted or doing other things when you are supposedly talking with them. Don't allow phones, beepers, e-mail alerts, or other people to interrupt this protected time.

- Less is more: People can't focus on too many issues at once. Center each discussion on one or two key topics at a time and build on these in later discussions.
- Be supportive: Make sure you are not coming across as intimidating or threatening when you offer suggestions. When you want something done in a certain way, make sure you explain what and why.

Tool 2
WORST CASE SCENARIO THINKING

One component in setting up a task should be engaging your coachee in identifying and anticipating roadblocks, so you can plan for them and often eliminate them or reduce their impact. This tool helps you identify the roadblocks to successful completion of the task or project you've delegated to your coachee.

- Ask the employee, "What do you think might get in your way or make this effort difficult for you?"
- After asking this open-ended question, dig for specifics by posing the following possible roadblocks and hearing out the employee's concerns:
  —Unclear goals and guidelines
  —Red tape
  —Not enough time
  —Lack of cooperation from others
  —Insufficient access to you for help and support
  —All criticism, no praise or appreciation
- Then address the concerns as well as you can at this early point. Here are a few tips related to these possible roadblocks.

If This Roadblock Is a Concern	Try This
Unclear goals and guidelines	Take pains to clarify the goals. How many times have you completed a project, produced the result, and then been told, "That's not what I wanted"? • What does the job or project entail? • Why is the job or project important? • How does the job fit into the big picture? • What do you expect the results to look like?

(Continued on next page)

Red tape	Eliminate red tape by proposing an alternative, or run interference. Clarify the employee's latitude to act. Options: • No tape: Just do it • Pink tape: Tell me what you did • Red tape: Get permission from me first • Duct tape: Forget it
Not enough time	• Negotiate; meet employees half way: Rearrange schedules, release people from a commitment, or take over a job of theirs, but don't leave people feeling overwhelmed. • Divide the project into small pieces.
Lack of cooperation from others	Pave the way: Make team aware of what person is doing and how it relates to the big picture. People need to feel responsible for each other's success. Help people talk about what they need from each other in order to accomplish the goal.

Insufficient access to you for help and support	• Be available
	• Tell people specific ways they can have access to you (e-mails, secretaries, voice mails, and closed doors can all be barriers).
	• Ask staff what they think blocks their access to you; do something about these.
	• Options:
	  —Announce clear office hours (e.g., three times per week minimum or during a specific hour daily).
	  —Post times during the week when staff can meet with you.
	  —Arrange clear and frequent check-in points (whether in writing or face to face, depending on what you and your staff prefer).
	  —Pick a project a week and give feedback to each person working on that project during that week.
	  —Ask people for feedback. Ask them to list things they view as "on target" or "giving them difficulty," and provide feedback to them about their list.

All criticism, no positive feedback	• Celebrate and praise: Talk about what's on target before you point out problems. • Write short, encouraging notes ("Keep up the good work!"). • Point out people's accomplishments in public forums. • Create a "wall of fame" bulletin board in your department. • Post thank-you letters. • Celebrate with a "halfway" or midpoint project lunch.

Tool 3
ENGAGING AN EXECUTIVE COACH

Under certain circumstances, one-on-one interaction with an objective third party can help leaders develop in a way other types of organizational support cannot. An executive coach can serve as an executive's truth speaker and conversation partner, preventing a feeling of "I'm in this alone" and serving as a sounding board for tough situations and decisions.

It used to be that executive coaches were employed to work with problem performers. These days, coaching is directed more often at top performers with the potential for future leadership. Coaching provides guidance and feedback in real time and develops people to excel in their current job without distracting them from their everyday responsibilities.

Many executives benefit from receiving feedback, since often they receive none at all, or the feedback they get is infrequent and unreliable because of their power. Many executives report a sense of isolation as they consider important decisions and actions. As people take on greater leadership, offer them development feedback or, even more basically, someone to talk to truthfully and privately with no chance of repercussions.

When is a coach especially helpful for you or the members of your team?

1. When you need a sounding board for your thinking
2. When you need help developing skills to make you more effective
3. In times of substantial change, such as mergers, acquisitions, stretch assignments, promotions, and role changes
4. When you need to get unstuck and refresh your approaches, develop new ways to attack old problems, or counter burnout

A big benefit of a coach is that the coach is in your corner, not connected to your organization, family, or friends. The coach is focused on supporting you exclusively.

Chapter 11

• • •

A Five-Point Plan
for Breakthroughs

*Executives need to lead with courage
and example if they are going to
overcome entrenched mind-sets.*

In my thirty-plus years as an executive, educator, consultant, change agent, and cancer patient, I have been privileged to meet many wonderful, dedicated people and engage with them in their quests to enhance the lives of patients, families, and their communities. After learning so much from so many, I want to share a few strongly held opinions with you as I bring this book to a close.

In my view, there are five *process changes* we as leaders need to make in order to expedite breakthroughs, whether we are seeking breakthroughs in the patient and family experience, quality and patient safety, employee satisfaction, financial health, or operational effectiveness. I am convinced that courageous leaders who have already accomplished these changes or who spearhead these process changes will strengthen their impact, reputation, and leadership legacy.

A Five-Point Plan for Expediting Breakthroughs

1. Institute zero tolerance of horizontal hostility and disrespect.
2. Stop diplomatic immunity.
3. Encourage difficult conversations.
4. Get real about the pressure, scrutiny, and challenges faced by frontline staff.
5. Repeatedly ask every member of your team select, transforming questions.

Institute Zero Tolerance of Horizontal Hostility and Disrespect

I'm talking about hostility and disrespect between co-workers and departments. Recent examples I've come across:

- "We can't keep a young nurse. Older nurses eat their young."
- "Nurses make cracks about me in front of patients all the time."
- "Those people in radiology never take people on time."
- Calling a housekeeper "Housekeeping!" instead of learning and using people's names.
- "Here they go again. They always. . . ."

As you know, hostility and disrespect—whether delivered with barbs, sneers, scowls, or gossip—play havoc with the patient and employee experience. I think we are far too tolerant, believing that the natural order of things—the pecking order—is at fault. Or perhaps it seems that some people deserve negative treatment because they often let their colleagues down. I think the time has come not only to acknowledge this as a serious issue but also to act on it, making the obliteration of horizontal hostility a housewide priority, communicating a zero-tolerance policy, training everyone in caring confrontation, and enforcing zero tolerance. Friction and interstaff disrespect infect relationships and make seamless service impossible.

Stop Diplomatic Immunity

Hold executives, not just frontline employees, to high standards of performance and respectful behavior. Is there a person or two on your executive team notorious for outrageous behavior or bullying—a so-called leader who makes people shake in their shoes? Is there an executive who causes others to consume their precious energies figuring out how to win their support or work around the obstacles they routinely create? If so, is it any wonder that employees faced with pressure to raise the bar in their own performance resist and sputter, "But what about Jim? He's awful to people and keeps getting the big bucks anyway!" or, "You expect me to treat people really well, but you should see my supervisor!"

It's time to hold our leadership colleagues and ourselves to the same standards we set for all staff. Many organizations spend thousands of dollars on 360-degree surveys to get data on executive performance problems, when, let's face it, everyone in the organization already knows exactly where the problems are. The survey becomes yet another delaying tactic or way to soft-pedal the truth—that the executive should make changes or leave.

Leaders rationalize when they hold onto problem executives: "But he's so good at finance, and it would be a bear to replace him!" The price you pay for double standards in morale and your team culture is enormous. Lay down the law to this person. If he or she has saving graces, provide a coach. Still, require the executive to make changes and *live* the organization's lofty values—or leave.

Encourage Difficult Conversations

Leaders are shielded from feedback. When the people reporting directly to you find you frustrating, they are unlikely to speak up about it. And if they think your leadership colleagues have made a misguided decision, a few might address this directly, but most will not. If a leader is notorious for inappropriate behavior, it's not unusual for employees to feel that this fact is unmentionable.

When you allow yourself to enjoy the fact that few are likely to disagree with you, give you negative feedback, or raise tough issues, you lose out on the healthy exchange that leads to the best possible decisions. You also miss opportunities to learn and grow. Also, unmentionables consume and drain people's energy, which you need to devote to creating a great patient experience and a healthy organization.

For the sake of your mission and your team, take steps to invite and encourage difficult conversations. Call speaking up *courageous*. Create a "safe container"—a time and place as well as ground rules that reduce the risk others take when they speak up. Make sure you and others do not create repercussions. And invest in training for yourself and all staff on how to hold difficult conversations caringly. The most highly respected leaders are the ones who make a concerted effort to reduce intimidation and fear and to initiate, nurture, and appreciate courageous conversation.

Get Real about the Pressure, Scrutiny, and Challenges Faced by Frontline Staff

From where we sit, it's easy to exhort people to provide great service to patients and families. But consider an outpatient service where the receptionist is responsible for meeting, greeting, registering, and directing patients while at the same time answering a phone that's ringing off the hook and scheduling appointments—all without causing anyone to feel impatient or disregarded. Add to that the fact that some patients and callers are distressed, demanding, or complaining. How can even the most motivated staff members accomplish their tasks quickly, communicate with kindness and empathy, and provide impeccable customer service to the people in front of them and the callers all at once?

Or consider the inpatient caregivers who are not only responsible for a whole host of tasks and requirements but also deal with distressed and sometimes difficult patients, families, and co-workers. Many, including absolutely wonderful employees, feel they are drowning in a burgeoning pool of expectations: Complete your tasks expertly. Learn new procedures quickly. Make no mistakes. Keep patients safe. Personalize the care. Respond quickly. Keep people informed. Ease the way of the doctors. Educate the patient and family. Help your co-workers. Show compassion. Communicate with empathy. Leave no stone unturned.

Visit those areas and see firsthand what life is like for the people on the front line. Shadow them. Listen to them. Perhaps some jobs are just undoable and need to be altered. For instance, how about having a staff dedicated to answering phones, while different staff serve people face to face? Or, if that's impossible, then at least acknowledge the people doing these harrowing jobs. Set reasonable expectations and show understanding, support, and respect. And recognize that when you add responsibilities and expectations, you make the job even more complex and pressure filled. Something's gotta give.

Repeatedly Ask Every Member of Your Team Select, Transforming Questions

With so many priorities on your plate and so much on the minds of staff, health care work can easily feel overwhelming. Is it any wonder that many people end up doing the job in a perfunctory way, exclaiming "TGIF!" when the end of their workweek finally arrives? It's a tragedy that so many wonderful people in health care cope with the pressure and multiple responsibilities by disconnecting from their original helping mission.

In my view, it is a pivotal responsibility of leaders to focus people. You've heard the line, "People respect what management inspects." If your questions and observations focus on finances, market share, business opportunity, satisfaction "scores," scorecard data, and the like, it's no wonder that people disconnect from their helping mission.

How about asking these questions—which focus your workforce on the patient and family experience, on their contribution, and on the meaning in their work—as a matter of routine:

- How have you shown loving care today?
- Tell me about a time when you felt privileged to do the work you do.
- How did you "pay it forward" today with co-workers?

Ask these questions one on one, in team meetings and huddles, and in performance review discussions. And make them the focus of celebrations, newsletters, e-mails, and recognition events.

Use Your Power to Set the Pace and Pave the Way

Gandhi said, "Be the change you want to create." To achieve breakthroughs in your organization, your example and your courageous leadership are pivotal. I hope this five-point plan sparks discussion with your team and triggers constructive, purposeful action.

Thanks very much for listening.

● ● ●

Additional Tools

Tool 1
THE "STOP DISRESPECT" CAMPAIGN

If employees complain about disrespect, whether it's disrespect from doctors, between departments, or between co-workers, consider adopting the organizationwide breakthrough objective "Wipe out disrespect." And conduct a campaign to advance this objective.

Key Campaign Components

1. In a managers' meeting, have leaders announce a zero-tolerance approach to disrespectful behavior. Enrich this by having individuals on the executive team make a statement of personal commitment to behaving respectfully and confronting disrespect in a respectful way.
2. Circulate a staff meeting plan for all managers to follow with their team.

Staff Meeting Plan

> - Share stories of respect and disrespect (without naming names).
> - After hearing some of these stories, brainstorm the "dos and don'ts of respect."

3. Provide a short skill-building module for all staff housewide on a respectful way to confront disrespect.
   —Make a pitch on a vision of a workplace in which respect flows throughout.
   —Present and engage people in practicing a language model for everyone to use to confront disrespect respectfully. Appeal to people to adopt this approach in order to get the best possible results.

Language Model for Confronting Disrespect

> "When you _____, I feel disrespected. When I feel disrespect from you, it's hard for me to support you."

And in the face of resistance or excuses, persist in your caring message, as follows:

You say	• "I know you care, and I want to support you." • "When you _____, I feel disrespected." • "It makes it hard for me to support you."	Explain your positive intent.
S/he says	"Yes, but _____."	The other person makes excuses or counterattacks.
You say	• "You might think that." • "I just want you to know that when I feel disrespect from you, it's hard for me to support you."	• Use "fogging" (say something accepting without agreeing or disagreeing). • Use the broken record (repeat your main point).

4. Institute a quarterly respect report card. Feed back the results to all managers, and at a management meeting, generate and plan the execution of a furthering respect action plan.

5. Create a respect recognition program through which every employee can issue respect telegrams to others when they experience or witness a respectful act that is particularly heartwarming.

6. Communicate fully with physicians about this campaign. Alert them to the language model that staff are being encouraged to use. Invite them to join in for the sake of patients and the team.

Tool 2
GETTING REAL ABOUT LIFE ON THE FRONT LINE: A QUICK INTERVIEW APPROACH

During rounding, consider doing five-minute interviews with two frontline employees each week to find out what their lives are like from their perspectives.

Introduction

I'm _____ and I'm making some rounds so I stay in close touch with how patients and our staff are experiencing our organization and services. I'd appreciate the chance to do a very brief interview with you—just five minutes—to learn a bit about what your life is like here. Are you willing to do that? Now, or can we set a time? I really appreciate it.

Questions

1. How would you describe a typical work day?
2. What are the most satisfying things you do in the course of a day?
3. What are the most frustrating things you do in the course of a day?
4. How do people on your team support each other?
5. If you could give your team a gift, what would that be?

Sample Closing

Thank you so much for talking with me. It's important to me to hear from the people who really do the work here. It will help me make better decisions and devote time to the right things. Here's my card in case you want to talk further or if I can help you in any way. Thanks again.

Appendix

• • •

Additional Resources
for Health Care Leaders

On Leadership

Ashkenas, R., Ulrich, D., Jick, T., and Kerr, S., *The Boundaryless Organization: Breaking the Chains of Organizational Structure* (San Francisco: Jossey-Bass, 2002).

Boyatzis, R., and McKee, A., *Resonant Leadership: Renewing Yourself and Connecting with Others through Mindfulness, Hope, and Compassion* (Cambridge, MA: Harvard Business School Press, 2005).

Collins, J., *Good to Great: Why Some Companies Make the Leap . . . And Others Don't* (New York: Collins, 2001).

Covey, S., *The 8th Habit Personal Workbook: Strategies to Take You from Effectiveness to Greatness* (New York: Free Press, 2006).

Gladwell, M., *The Tipping Point: How Little Things Can Make a Big Difference* (New York: Back Bay Books, 2002).

Goleman, D., *Primal Leadership: Learning to Lead with Emotional Intelligence* (Cambridge, MA: Harvard Business School Press, 2002).

Henly, K., "Detoxifying a Toxic Leader," *Innovative Leader* (June 2003).

Hunt, J., and Weintraub, J., *The Coaching Manager: Developing Top Talent in Business* (Thousand Oaks, CA: Sage Publications, 2002).

Kotter, J., *Leading Change* (Cambridge, MA: Harvard Business School Press, 1996).

Kouzes, J., and Posner, B., A Leader's Legacy (San Francisco: Jossey-Bass, 2006).

Leebov, W., and Scott, G., *Health Care Managers in Transition: Shifting Roles and Changing Organizations* (San Francisco: Jossey-Bass, 1990).

Leebov, W., and Scott, G., *The Indispensable Health Care Manager: Success Strategies for a Changing Environment* (San Francisco: Jossey-Bass, 2002).

Sanborn, M., "*The Fred Factor: How Passion in Your Work and Life Can Turn the Ordinary into the Extraordinary* (New York: Currency, 2004).

Whicker, M., *Toxic Leaders: When Organizations Go Bad* (Westport, CT: Quorum Books, 1996).

On Time and Priority Management

Bossidy, L., Charam, R., and Burck, C., *Execution: The Discipline of Getting Things Done* (New York: Crown Business, 2002).

Covey, S., Merrill, A. R., and Merrill, R. R., *First Things First: To Live, to Love, to Learn, to Leave a Legacy* (New York: Free Press, 1996).

Linenberger, M., *Total Workday Control Using Microsoft Outlook: The Eight Best Practices of Task and E-Mail Management* (San Ramon, CA: New Academy Publishers, 2006).

Morgenstern, J., *Time Management from the Inside Out: The Foolproof System for Taking Control of Your Schedule—and Your Life* (New York: Owl Books, 2004).

Neiman, R., *Execution Plain and Simple: Twelve Steps to Achieving Any Goal On Time and On Budget* (New York: McGraw-Hill, 2004).

On Leading Change

Conger, J., Spreitzer, G., and Lawler, E., *The Leader's Change Handbook: An Essential Guide to Setting Direction and Taking Action* (San Francisco: Jossey-Bass, 1998).

Gandossy, R., Verma, N., and Tucker, E., *Workforce Wake-up Call: Your Workforce Is Changing. Are You?* (New York: John Wiley, 2006).

Schmeling, W., *Facing Change in Health Care: Learning Faster in Tough Times* (Chicago: AHA Press, 1996).

Schwartz, P., *The Art of the Long View: Planning for the Future in an Uncertain World* (New York: Currency, 1996).

Seligman, M., *Learned Optimism: How to Change Your Mind and Your Life* (New York: Vintage, 2006).

Senge, P., Kleiner, A., Roberts, C., Ross, R., and Smith, B., *The Fifth Discipline Fieldbook* (New York: Currency, 1994).

Senge, P., Kleiner, A., Roberts, C., and Roth, G., *The Dance of Change: The Challenges to Sustaining Momentum in Learning Organizations* (New York: Currency, 1999).

Wheatley, M., *Turning to One Another: Simple Conversations to Restore Hope to the Future* (San Francisco: Berrett-Koehler, 2002).

On Relationships and Communication

Aguilar, L., "OUCH! That Stereotype Hurts," a powerful video on how to confront hurtful co-worker comments (available at www.learncom.com/index.do).

Bartholomew, K., *Ending Nurse-to-Nurse Hostility: Why Nurses Eat Their Young and Each Other* (Marblehead, MA: HCPro, 2006).

Cooper, R., and Sawaf, A., *Executive E.Q.: Emotional Intelligence in Leadership and Organization* (New York: Perigee Trade, 1998).

Fisher, R., Patton, B., and Ury, W., *Getting to Yes: Negotiating Agreement Without Giving In* (Boston: Houghton Mifflin, 1992).

Jones, R., "Conceptual Development of Nurse-Physician Collaboration," *Holistic Nurse Practice* 8 (3): 1–11 (1994).

Kramer, M., and Schmalenberg, C., "Securing Good Nurse Physician Relationships," *Nursing Management* (July 2003).

Leebov, W., *Assertiveness Skills for Healthcare Professionals* (Lincoln, NE: iUniverse, 2003).

Maurer, R., *Feedback Toolkit: 16 Tools for Better Communication in the Workplace* (New York: Productivity Press, 1994).

Neuhauser, P., *Tribal Warfare in Organizations: Turning Tribal Conflict into Negotiated Peace* (New York: Collins, 1990).

Paterson, R., *The Assertiveness Workbook: How to Express Your Ideas and Stand Up for Yourself at Work and in Relationships* (Oakland, CA: New Harbinger Publications, 2000).

Patterson, K., Grenny, J., McMillan, R., and Switzler, A., *Crucial Conversations: Tools for Talking when Stakes Are High* (New York: McGraw-Hill, 2002).

Reichheld, F., *Loyalty Rules! How Today's Leaders Build Lasting Relationships* (Cambridge, MA: Harvard Business School Press, 2003).

Scott, S., *Fierce Conversations: Achieving Success at Work and in Life One Conversation at a Time* (New York: Berkley Trade, 2004).

Stone, D., Patton, B., Heen, S., and Fisher, R., *Difficult Conversations: How to Discuss What Matters Most* (New York: Penguin, 2000).

On Enhancing the Patient Experience

Baker, S. K., *Managing Patient Expectations: The Art of Finding and Keeping Loyal Patients* (San Francisco: Jossey-Bass, 1998).

Beeson, S., *Practicing Excellence: A Physician's Manual to Exceptional Health Care* (Gulf Breeze, FL: Fire Starter Publishing, 2006).

Bergeson, S. C., and Dean, J. D., "A Systems Approach to Patient-Centered Care," *Journal of the American Medical Association* 296 (23): 2848–51 (2006).

Berwick, D., Godfrey, A. B., and Roessner, J., *Curing Health Care: New Strategies for Quality Improvement* (San Francisco: Jossey-Bass, 2002).

Berwick, D., Wasson, J. H., et al., "Technology for Patient-Centered, Collaborative Care," *Journal of Ambulatory Care Management* 47 [special issue] (June 22, 2006).

Conway, J., Johnson, B., Edgman-Levitan, S., et al., "Partnering with Patients and Families to Design a Patient- and Family-Centered Health Care System: A Roadmap for the Future," unpublished report from the Institute for Healthcare Improvement, available for free download from www.IHI.org.

Frampton, S., Gilpin, L., and Charmel, P., *Putting Patients First: Designing and Practicing Patient-Centered Care* (San Francisco: Jossey-Bass, 2003).

Gerteis, M., Edgman-Levitan, S., Daley, J., and Delbanco, T., eds., *Through the Patient's Eyes: Understanding and Promoting Patient-Centered Care* (San Francisco: Jossey-Bass, 1993).

Institute for Patient and Family-Centered Care, "Advancing the Practice of Patient- and Family-Centered Care: How to Get Started," unpublished report, available for free download from www.familycenteredcare.org.

Institute for Patient and Family-Centered Care, "Hospitals Moving Forward with Family-Centered Care," unpublished report, available for free download from www.familycenteredcare.org.

Joint Commission, *Patients as Partners: How to Involve Patients and Families in Their Own Care* (Oak Brook Terrace, IL: Joint Commission Resources, 2006).

Lee, F., *If Disney Ran Your Hospital: 9 1/2 Things You Would Do Differently* (Bozeman, MT: Second River Healthcare, 2004).

Leebov, W., Afriat, S., and Presha, J., *Service Savvy Health Care: One Goal at a Time* (Chicago: AHA Press, 1998).

Leebov, W., and Scott, G., *Service Quality Improvement: The Customer Satisfaction Strategy for Health Care* (Lincoln, NE: Authors Choice Press, 2007).

Leebov, W., Scott, G., and Olson, L., *Achieving Impressive Customer Service: Strategies for the Health Care Manager* (Chicago: AHA Press, 1998).

Press, I., *Patient Satisfaction: Understanding and Managing the Experience of Care* (Chicago: Health Administration Press, 2005).

Stubblefield, A., *The Baptist Healthcare Journey to Excellence: Creating a Culture that WOWs!* (New York: John Wiley, 2004).

Studer, Q., *Hardwiring Excellence: Purpose, Worthwhile Work, Making a Difference* (Gulf Breeze, FL: Fire Starter Publishing, 2004).

Index